To steal *a* moment's time

A Memoir

Katharina Berger
WITH G.J. Berger

FROM THE TINY ACORN ...
GROWS THE MIGHTY OAK

www.AcornPublishingLLC.com

For information, address:
Acorn Publishing, LLC
3943 Irvine Blvd. Ste. 218
Irvine, CA 92602

To Steal a Moment's Time

Cover design by Damonza.com
Interior design and formatting by Debra Cranfield Kennedy

Printed in the United States of America

ISBN-13: 979-8-88528-068-6 (hardcover)
ISBN-13: 979-8-88528-067-9 (paperback)
Library of Congress Control Number (LCCN): 2023912073

To All Mothers—everywhere.

If all mothers had a voice, war would cease.

TABLE OF CONTENTS

PREFACE

Düsseldorf, Germany, 1944

When Katharina heard the whistling, she knew it meant death. *Not now. I must live—for the new life growing inside me.*

In recent years, even earlier today, theatregoers had stood in lines circling city blocks to see her, their star and leading lady. But on this night, she sensed that soon she and they would all stand in longer lines for spongy potatoes or a loaf of stale bread.

She began to pray aloud. Other voices joined in, all trying to pray over the inferno up on the streets. At one of the stronger shakes, the lone candle went out.

Later, after the bomb rage had passed and those with her in the cellar had scurried away, she sat alone at the edge of a fountain in a park. She soaked her scarf in the fountain's warm water and hung it over her hair. She looked back to the street and the Guest House where she had a room.

She stared.

And stared.

Structures on the entire street lay flat, all of them but for that Guest House. It stood narrow and tall without windows, like a chimney on hot ashes and rubble. The houses on this stretch had abutted each other until the bomb raid that very night. A miracle, she thought.

Beautiful musical notes drifted in from somewhere close. Katharina wondered if she had gone mad, if her hearing had blown out with everything around her. In all this chaos, music?

Dazed, she staggered to low bushes still standing.

Nightingales on the ash-covered branches welcomed in the morning.

Katharina wept.

Born to high-end porcelain shop owners in a Bavarian village in 1910, Katharina left home at age sixteen for Munich, where she found an independent life on stage and in motion pictures. In those times, every city, many towns, and provinces operated government-supported theatres. Year-round they presented classics from Shakespeare, Goethe, Ibsen, and others, along with more current plays. Ironically, Hitler continued to support plays from the small-town operations to grand state-sponsored productions in major cities. But Katharina despised every aspect of Hitler and the Nazi movement, refused to salute when all around her did, helped Jews escape or warned them to not come home. As World War II raged ever closer and began to crush ordinary civilians, Katharina found the love of her life, a German radio announcer and writer. Later, she became pregnant. This is her story during the tumultuous first year of her son's life, as recorded by her in journals and diaries and later translated from the original German.

Part I

A Newborn
in a
Time of War

Katharina as Lady Milford
in Shiller's
Kabale und Liebe (*Cabal and Love*)

1

Winter's Nest

Kladow, Near Berlin, January 3, 1945

In the baby chamber, my dear baby boy was crying. I carefully turned him onto his side, and he fell asleep at once.

Yes, I have a son. His name is Georg, after his father.

Enthralled, I stood there in front of his Betti (little bed), observing, looking. Looking at his mouth so daintily formed, his sleeping eyes covered by web-lashed eyelids, his crooked little nose. His high forehead topped by short light hairs, silky, like sunbeams through a winter forest. I already comb them with a white brush. His tiny, perfectly-designed hands stretching like those of a Malayan dancer, and they are asleep too.

"See, my son, thus you lie in your kingdom without a notion of the war crushing in, of the madness. May we come through this," I whisper and wish.

Today he is two months old.

I've decided to write it down. Later, when he is a grown man and I might have the fortune to still be alive, I will no longer remember one thing or another. I will, therefore, whenever I am able to steal a moment's time, record what is happening with us and around us while he is becoming accustomed to life—to this life which seems to offer little more than death.

The diapers still soak in the bathtub. Yes, we have a bathroom. Small, narrow, I can hardly turn around, but what privilege to have a bathroom. One used to be able build a fire underneath the bath oven and make hot water, but no longer. Charcoal briquettes have disappeared.

The dishes are piled up in the kitchen, and many well-worn clothes are piled up in the basket to be sewn and ironed.

It is very cold. Below freezing. A clear sparkling winter day. The fire in the stove here is going out. I can't rekindle it now. Not enough wood left, must save the few pieces we have for the baby chamber. He has to keep warm.

Quickly, quickly, more tomorrow.

January 4, 1945

There's our morning bell. The milkman is ringing outside. I'll rush.

I receive a quarter litre of milk every day because I have a baby. The milkman brings it in a large carriage drawn by an old thin horse. I can count its ribs. All mothers in this neighborhood run to him to not dare miss him. He is supposed to come every other day, but lately has missed many days.

We have a milk card, clipped for every quarter litre. It allows my son to grow, to stay alive. We also have a card for corn-flour and one for soap. They are red, blue, and green. We can only get these things with cards because people are waging war. Yes, these cards have greater value than money or jewels.

How I would like to drink the milk in one gulp. Grownups

don't get any. But mothers don't take . . . they only give.

While I was gone, Georg began to cry terribly. I heard him the entire way. I rushed back. But everything seemed to be all right. He was dry, had had his bottle, just cranky because of the air-raid alarms.

There was one at dawn today, and it took him by surprise while fast asleep—as too often. He looked quite wide-eyed at this incredible undertaking of quickly being wrapped in blankets and pulled out of the warmth into the freezing laundry room down in the cellar. It is our bomb shelter. His blue eyes, shaped like almonds, show amazement. His brows, faint rosy indications, drew themselves together as with grown-ups.

———————————

Another alarm sounded late in the evening, long after winter darkness.

If I only had a carriage. The Magistrate's Office must process the permit. That misguided word—process. It means many men investigate whether I have a son here on this earth, whether he really needs a carriage. They can't process together, must do their processing one at a time.

Drudgery at every alarm. In one arm two large bags with necessities to eat, to wear. In the other arm the blanket bundle.

This trembling whenever the planes roar over and around us. Whenever I hear them, I can't stop my trembling.

If I had a carriage, I could prepare. First put baby to sleep in it, carefully lift it down the stairs without waking him. Bags with our most essential items would fit by his side. And he would sleep right through.

Today it was trying. Four families, Nazis, assigned to our

laundry room shelter, chatted through all the anti-aircraft shooting as if nothing were amiss. They said in one breath that from now on, one has the privilege to obtain an air-bed for babies from the magistrate. Proudly stressing "privilege." I almost screamed. But I must not give myself away.

Good night, my little son. Sleep. Your mother is watching over you. How many lullabies end like this? Mothers have never watched as now.

I am so tired.

January 5, 1945

Beautiful hand-woven green drapes hang in Georg's window. Something of our own left over after Mommy's former house burned to the ground with many wonderful things. It was the second house Mommy lost to this war. But I won't write about that, not now, not today. No sense in that.

On the walls hang many pictures with deer and dwarves. Papa glued them onto strips of black paper. Frames are no longer available. There is a big green-tiled stove and next to it a table on which baby gets changed, cleaned and weighed. On which he kicks off diapers and laughs and babbles.

This table is age-old and has wobbly legs. I bartered Papa's last cigarette ration for it. It came from only up the street but took me half an hour to carry it home. The whole thing fell apart on the way. Then you have your own brand-new white Betti, which Papa hauled through all of Berlin on the last day of his short leave. I live in the other two upstairs rooms.

I don't often see the people who rent downstairs but hear their radio at night. A man and two women, all middle-aged. The man must be on leave or have high Nazi connections to not be on the front or in a factory. In these times, strangers keep to themselves, and I can't bear to be around them. Though when we do see each other, I wave at them and make small talk. They've never asked about you or tried to look at you.

Our house is part of a small settlement of about forty houses. Nests in the bare birch trees dot the gray sky and make me wonder how much longer our little nest here will last. We are an hour's bus ride from the city of Berlin. Bus runs are getting less reliable. Peaceful pines, birches, fields, and a lake frame these houses. A boat passage across the lake and then train connection get far into the city, but this too is sporadic.

The Russian army is advancing on the far side of Berlin. The Americans are closing in from the West. I pray the Americans get here before the Russians.

2

Closing In

January 7, 1945

Night. Two o'clock.

I lean against the window. It is icy and cold outside. I send my thoughts out there into the freezing world. Ten minutes ago, we came up out of the cellar. Georg scolded.

In the distance over Berlin, flashes of fire, and the bright white streaks of planes all the way to over our house. An icy, jingling world on fire. There is so much madness. If I can remain sane?

Beneath us the radio blares even now. Operetta music broken by the position reports of the departing bombers. The stations won't turn off for the night until the planes are over the English Channel. My baby fell asleep in spite of it. And the dance music goes on and on—waltzing with death.

Mozart played a lot on the radio today—interrupted by hymns of praise for the newly-invented V-I Waffe (weapon). Then the radio broadcast a Beethoven concerto with children's chorus, broadcast from an armament factory, from the same halls in which rows of tanks coldly, proudly await their missions. Oh, my son.

On Christmas Eve, an air raid struck Vienna. The Operahaus and Burgtheater were destroyed. The same night, the radio blared out a famous Viennese tune: *So spielen die Geiger nur in Wien* (Violins play like this only in Vienna).

Alarm! Again.

They must be coming back. Poor little boy. I'll wait a bit longer. But when the radio says the planes are over Magdeburg, we must rush down once more.

January 9, 1945

I remember a picture of a white house with pillars on a mountain top. On one side a throng of old weary people pulled themselves up the mountain road to the house. They emerged from the other side young, handsome, invigorated. I go into the baby-chamber like those people. I too come back out renewed. There must be a newborn in that white house.

Georg slept through until eight in the morning. At nine he fell asleep again.

It is noon. Two little eyes look over the huge white cover as if over a wall. Little hand clutches my finger, and he begins to tell me everything with delightful "ahs."

I understand what you are telling me: sleep is so wonderful, you are warm and comfortable, and a bottle is expected . . .

Nothing must happen to you. I will be alert.

January 10, 1945

Night, 12 o'clock.

Up from the cellar. It was terrible, the whistling of the bombs. They build whistles into them to frighten anyone near the strike.

These kinds of bombs do not need whistles. Blockbusters. Sleep now, my baby . . . I will pray that we may sleep through what remains of this night.

January 11, 1945

I just came back with the milk.

Oh, my son. I don't know how to begin.

Frau Meier, who was here in your room only days ago, who looked at you and said, "He'll pull through. He is in fine shape now." That's what she said about you.

Today Frau Meier didn't come for her milk. And there was no sign of her daughter either, nor of her happy little boy . . . and they said there is a crater instead of her house. All the women around the milk wagon were paler than usual. We all ran back home faster than on other days.

January 12, 1945

Ice-wind-diaper-orgy!

The diapers freeze to boards in the attic. When I get them down and lean them against the oven, the diaper-boards thaw instead of dry. Gas has been locked off. Hotplates are forbidden too. I still use our tiny electric cooking plate. I can't obey. I secretly cook Georg's porridge, warm his bottle, boil his diapers, a few at a time, and heat water for his bath—in many portions.

Am waiting for a letter . . . Our local post office is still operating, standing. Mail still makes it around Germany.

———————————

An unexpected visitor, our landlady. When the air raids began, she moved east into the country to her father's farm.

Suddenly, she stood there in the room this morning. She has a key.

I had my radio on rather loudly. If she had noticed that I was listening to the wrong station, the peace in our kingdom would have been over. It's a foreign sender. Listening to it is forbidden under penalty of prison. Death. Neighbors, even friends, report on each other.

My knees shook as I turned it off and loudly offered her some corn-coffee to mask the radio reports.

No one dares to talk to anyone. I lock up this notebook.

We rented the apartment with its furniture from this woman, because I had been through *Fliegerangriff* (air-attack) and *Bombenschaden* (damage from bombs) in the west, in Aachen. Two bad words. Their definitions include fear, poverty, and dependence . . . no chair, no table, no bed, nothing, not a toothbrush remained from my last house. Only your chamber still has those green drapes and little bed of our own.

God keep these for us.

The landlady drank coffee and chatted of "our victory." She packed up a few things, went into the cellar to collect her jars of home-made preserves. Pears, cherries in rows. The display has become familiar. How often do I stand there in the cellar and touch these wonders? So terribly tempted to open them . . . sick with hunger.

January 15, 1945

Late at night.

We were in the cellar three times. Everything is in chaos. Baby's last meal was at eleven at night. And now he is coughing. And the radio downstairs blares and blares again of . . . RESERVES . . . of the new ones who are being thrown into the battle . . . of the old ones who are exhausted.

Reserves. Those are men, my son, like you shall become. Leaders call up reserves when the regular fighters can't handle what they must, what the leaders command them to do. May you never belong to "Reserves." I will pray that I will never have to weep as the many mothers who now must offer their most loved and who once stood in front of the bed and watched their sleeping child.

I am writing Papa now and telling him how we are. I will tell him that we love him and remain brave.

January 16, 1945

I had to run to the post office. There I met Kati Bard, a colleague. She works in an armament factory. All theatres have been closed since August. Actors are on the front. Actresses work in factories. Only she who has a baby may stay home.

At the post office sat a package from your aunt in the mountains of Austria. I tore it open in the woods on the way home. A dust cloth, two rolls of fine paper, four apples. Things which have long not existed. The apples were a bit spoiled, but I ate them on the spot.

January 17, 1945

A letter from our Papa! Your father is a roaming radio announcer. Sometimes, they assign him to report right from the front.

He says he is well and far back from the fighting. He is not allowed to say where he is but says it's not far from us. He may get a few days leave soon and will try to find us. He says he loves us.

Now I have courage again. Even in the cellar.

January 18, 1945

The gift of life. When one watches over, when one cares for one's own baby. Mothers who are able to do this unearth the world's treasure.

On good days, care starts between six and eight every morning. First the bottle. Then washing and creaming on our wobbly table. Cleaning eyes and nose. Georg smiles at this, and that always makes me smile back.

Every third day at eleven a wonderful bath with water heated in small batches on our secret cooking plate. Then precious carrot juice. What a mess preparing it. It tests my patience. First grating, then squeezing through a linen napkin. That takes such a long time, but medicine in every drop. I have heard of ready-made carrot juice for babies in America. Well, so long as we can get carrots we are lucky.

When there is no cold wind, I carry my son in the laundry basket down to the yard behind the house. But today a snowstorm swept large happy snowflakes into the window gap as soon as I opened it just a bit. I shielded him with a sheet, and his clear eyes looked puzzled at the thin canopy. Ice gnomes are at work too, painting beautiful ice flowers on the window.

After the bath, my son sleeps for many hours. In the afternoon another cleaning and bottle time, then sleep again until eight.

Thus passes a good day if alarms do not disrupt everything.

In between I often hurry to the grocer, a half hour run-walk through the forest, through glittering, ice covered-birches. I worry the entire way. The alarms are so unpredictable. I tightly hold onto the little booklet with the colored food ration stamps. If a line has formed in front of the store, something good is being given out.

Perhaps a pound of sugar, margarine, or even a half pound of noodles, and that is then wonderful.

January 20, 1945

Five hundred bombers attacked Leipzig yesterday, one thousand Dresden and Magdeburg. In the east the Russians move steadily closer. They have taken Litzmannstadt, Neidenburg, Krakow. The Americans press hard from the West.

But I? I am happy. Why? Because the sun shone today? No, much more than that, and soon my son will share my happiness. I have some peace now and will write a story for him.

3

How We Got a Carriage

Once upon a time a woman bore a child. It was a son. At the time
men flew, flew high above the earth, above clouds in huge bird-like
machines. And from their birds they threw fire down with a horrible
clamor, killing men and animals, destroying huts and palaces,
bridges and cathedrals, destroying all the beautiful things which
they had built and loved.

The woman trembled with fear, her hidden child too. He
wanted to know what had happened and came into the open one
month before his secret growing had been finished—naked, tiny,
and crying. Whenever the fire came down from the sky so noisily, he
cried bitterly and couldn't stop crying.

Men had also created the most beautiful carriages for their
newborns, rocking baskets with lace and silk linings, all riding on
noiseless wheels. But now these were broken and burned with
houses and everything in them. Only ersatz items remained, substi-
tutions for everything decent and good.

The woman tried to get an ersatz carriage.

She walked many streets, up many stairs, showed papers to many important men. The papers said a son really and truly had been born to her. One man gave the papers to another. And then to another in another room, and then again to another. All the men sat silently behind huge desks and all looked sternly at her until she dared to ask, "Are you the gentleman with the carriage?"

At last one man smiled back and said, "I am the one. You may have it."

"The carriage?" the woman said.

"The certificate," said the man.

Now the woman had the certificate with a stamp and a seal! And on it was written, "The owner is permitted to purchase a carriage, if she can find one."

At once the woman began to search. She searched for three days. She rode along tracks, under streets, above them, and around in the big city. And she asked here and there, and all of a sudden, she found it.

On the fourth day, a strange woman told her where she could get it, exactly where.

The woman went out again. She put on make-up as back then when there was no war. She painted her lips red. She went down into the cellar, uncovered her fur and wrapped herself in it. She would never forget this day.

On the street to the train station, she saw her husband. Yes, after four months he unexpectedly came heading home out of his desolation, away from the wounded earth and bleeding men at his post as their radio announcer.

"For a few hours," he said when they were close.

In the train they were able to sit together. They didn't speak but both smiled. At last the woman said, "I have a certificate for our son's carriage. Now, we'll get it together."

"Yes," said the man.

The compartment was crowded. People looked at the woman with the painted red lips and the silvery fur. Bitter, pensive, jealous. At first, the woman didn't see their looks. She felt warm, at home with the man at her side. Later thinking back, she wondered if some in the crowd recognized her. She should not have put on makeup for this special trip, better to blend in.

They found the building, once a great store with lights everywhere, a huge, black ruin with walls and pillars bent and burned, with staircases dark and damp.

The man and woman climbed the stairs. They stopped and looked up, up along a deep crater, a split building, up to the clouds grey and heavy. The uppermost staircase swayed but led to a room with a light.

And there the woman spotted three, yes, three carriages. She burst into laughter, took one and drove it up and down until a sharp voice stopped her. "Don't touch! Only with a certificate."

"We have. Triplicate certificates have we," she said to the old pale man.

With this magic paper the parents purchased a white carriage and received more surprises. The pale man found them a wooden stand for drying diapers, a pan, and a dish. These needed no certificate.

Her husband carried their goods down the swaying stairs, one step at a time, balancing, waiting, leaning, but they made it to firm ground.

"Look. A star," said the woman.

"The roof is gone," said the man and looked up. "The star is directly over us."

"It greets the carriage."

The streets now black, they couldn't see each other. People scurried and coughed and rustled around them. Man's greatest invention, light, extinguished. Though the carriage shined, a white boat on black water.

"Hungry," said the woman, "Terribly hungry."

The good days when one might have tasted sweet peaches, yellow pears, shiny grapes left them years before, their memory flitting in like fairy tales. Back then, the man would have said, "Come! Over there is the Drachenstube. We'll get something and a bottle of red wine. They have the best wine in all of Berlin. Come."

Today, only a wooden hut sits over there. Dark figures stream in and out of it.

The man squeezed the carriage through the small door, and both entered.

Instantly the woman felt and saw that she was the only woman amidst a frightening crowd of rough-looking men, dirty men, as though they lived in caves and had just come out. All of them stared at the woman and then at the carriage. They talked to each other, furtively in subdued voices and in strange tongues. The woman gripped her white treasure and didn't look up.

Right then she didn't know—from whence could she know—that these men, these dark creatures, were not evil, only sick, homesick. Destitute and worn out. They had been torn away from treasures like a baby carriage, from love and from home. Their homes were Hitler's conquered states: France, Hungary, Bulgaria ... They had been driven into freight trains with whips, had been forced to slavery in munitions factories for the Third Reich and treated like beasts. This little hut was their only haven.

After a time, the man came back from the counter carefully balancing something over the people's heads. Sausages and beer! Yes, beer! It was ersatz beer, but the first sip tasted real. The sausages were made of cabbage, ersatz meat, and wrapped in red paper, but good, so good.

"Now, home," they said in one breath.

———

At the platform, chains locked the big gate to the train. At a smaller entrance a woman punched tickets. She wore heavy men's clothing. "Stop. Carriages without babies can't pass."

"Why not?"

"Regulations."

A dense, shouting mob behind them threatened to crush the carriage. You had better watch out, little carriage! Help yourself! Look around! There, over there is another gate. Tuck down your cover, squeeze under the chain, and right into the train.

The woman found a seat, and the man lifted the white wonder up onto a shelf somewhere in the crowded coupe.

"As long as there is always another gate," said the woman. Rain whipped onto the blacked-out windows. Trees hushed by ghostlike. Eight stations. Nine. Before the last stop a voice shouted, *"Alles austeigen! Flieger Alarm!"* (Everybody out! Airplane alarm!)

The man carried the carriage down many stairs, down to some unknown street. A rushing throng almost pushed him over. Where can they find shelter? No one answered. They followed the others, already accompanied by planes grumbling, to an entrance of a cave.

21

The carriage had to remain outside, lonely and lost in the rain as though already discarded.

The cave was black, wet and crowded. Hard and close detonations.

"It's better when you are here," the woman whispered.

Will . . . will at home . . . will everything be all right at home, she thought.

Shrill sounds penetrated everything and everyone, the all-clear signal, sirens of relief—or of death.

They all climbed out of the cave. Millions of citizens of the great Third Reich climbed out of ditches, bunkers and cellars, obedient and trembling. Some stayed in their shelters forever.

The train did not go on. The man and woman had to march to a lake, a pier, from where they might catch the last boat to the other side.

The way was dark and drizzling, and the woman was tired. "Perhaps this life, granted each day anew, perhaps this too is grace," she mumbled.

The carriage rolled along, a bit squeaky, but it rolled with the pan and the dish the pale man had given them. They rattled, but that was a good sound.

They found the pier but had to wait. Each breath made a white cloud in the cold air.

"Go into that house, there along the shore," said the man. "Perhaps you can warm yourself."

The house was a tavern, with a lighted and warm beer-hall where chairs were set up in rows as if for a movie. Many men came into the hall. The woman pressed herself into a corner. The men wore brown suits embroidered with thick golden stars. They marched in silently and filled the hall. Some carried red banners, waved them back and forth.

They all snapped to attention, in unison lifted their right arms, and sang out, *"Es gehört uns die ganze Welt."* (The whole world belongs to us.)

One of the men with shiny black boots stepped onto a small stool and declared how good, how grand, how stupendous the present time is, how good, how great they themselves were.

The woman left. She had seen this ritual of a major with his men before. She went back to the pier and felt the cold even more.

There in the fog, a long line had formed, winding and dark. A monotone voice said, "You can have it . . . the house . . . the garden . . . apple trees . . . all, if you give me your radio." The voice lied, tried to get a precious radio worth much more than the voice had to offer. Tricks, fraud everywhere.

Shouting voices. "The ship is coming! It's coming." A light pierced the fog. It grew brighter and suddenly dazzlingly bright. The boat swallowed all, the black snake of people waiting, the man, the woman and the carriage.

Again, they had to climb and push, this time onto the glass roof over the engine room. Up there, the carriage shook its way over the water.

The man held the woman's cold hand. Their greenish faces reflected the light from the engine room below.

When they were across, the rain had stopped. They trudged home through the birch woods, feeling their way over the roots in darkness. The man steered the carriage with one hand, supported the woman with the other. Raindrops fell off the branches onto her cheeks, or were they tears?

"Soon we'll be home," the man said quietly.

At home their son was asleep. Peacefully. A small light was still on and the oven still warm. The woman from next door, who had watched over him, awaited them.

There it stands now, the white carriage, and gives the whole room glory, though it is made only of cardboard and tin.

That ends the story of how we got your carriage.

4

Sacrifices, Large and Small

January 21, 1945

Another sub-zero day, but beautiful. Mom and Dad drove their son around in the new carriage.

An icy sun squinted through the pines spinning its long white webs of light onto the fields. But our dear little son didn't want to know anything of the world. Buried deep in his pillows he slept and slept. We couldn't see him without pulling his pillows off. My beloved husband must leave early tomorrow.

January 22, 1945

Alone again . . . Oh, no, I am not alone. My sleeping prince is with me, out in the fresh icy air in the backyard. I went down to him, just looked at him, a gift on this sad day of parting. The blue bonnet ribbon covered his little face. I straightened it out. Every time I went down, the blue ribbon lay across his face.

He had a bath today. And he told me more than ever before and not a single tear.

The lady from across the street came over. She has lost her

husband in this war, the father of two little girls. Holding back tears, she told me that all widows had been called upon to sacrifice the clothes of their fallen husbands "for the great victory."

"From his winter coat I've made a coat for one of the girls. It isn't much. I wish I could keep them?" she said.

January 25, 1945

Last night in the cellar was dreadful. A block-buster hit right next to us. I knelt on the ground bowed over my son. I couldn't pray. A soldier on leave dared to stay outside, but hustled back, pale. "It's better on the front," he said after a long while. I don't know the front he came from and never saw him again.

We had a visit from Nurse Else, our community nurse. She spread apples and nuts onto the table. I haven't seen nuts in six years. She always comforted me while I waited for my baby to arrive. And now she brings these small treasures.

Exhausted and drawn she fell into a chair. "Three babies came into this world last night. Scared from the bombs. They all came too early. I ran from one birth to the next."

On duty the entire night while death was all around her, and now she's helping me just through her presence.

Schwester (Sister) Else tells me of a blockbuster ... There are heaps of rubble in place of houses, right at the corner three blocks over. They pulled out six people. Another of them came for milk only yesterday.

Else rode her bicycle through the night, through snowstorm and sleet, to the only doctor in the area for a mother who needed help. As usual, all telephones were locked off after the attack. She fell to her knees begging him to come. "The woman will bleed to death.

Every minute counts," she cried at him. But it didn't help. The doctor refused and stomped out to his army vehicle. Then it occurred to her lie, to say, "She is the wife of a colonel."

"It's all the same," said the doctor. "Only soldiers count," and drove off.

She took a close look at my son. "His tummy is cramped from the irregular schedule. He urgently needs Vigantol (a Vitamin D preparation) and carrots. As many as you can get."

Carrots are becoming more and more difficult to find, and ours have long been used up.

Oh, this war! But our house is still standing. We must be grateful.

January 27, 1945

Our neighbor and her two little girls will watch over Georg. I must hurry to Berlin while buses and trains still go there. I must find carrots and Vigantol. And whatever I can find to eat.

Late in the evening

The clock downstairs is striking . . . ten . . . eleven. But I must write how it was in the big city.

Strange, I thought, while walking along the Kurfürstendamm, "I have a son." I felt slim and beautiful and a little proud. Also, there was no alarm the entire day!

5

The Big City, Now and Then

The Kurfürstendamm was once the most interesting boulevard in Berlin. Now, a street of ruins, overrun by soldiers, wounded, bandaged and many on crutches. And women, displaying their elegant clothes, hats, furs, suits, shoes. All are gifts from their high Nazi friends. Strange elegance from Paris. Items from the newly conquered States of the Third Reich. Then the mobs clinging to restaurant windows, lurking, hungry. Some windows display greenish-red tarts, the colors of IG Farben, a world-famous paint factory.

I once lived there on the Kurfürstendamm. Today I stood in front of the house again. Only the facade is left. Behind it—emptiness. At the very top used to sit a balcony, my balcony. And I recalled a sultry September evening five years ago.

From that balcony I looked at the haze hanging over the boulevard into an uninhabited darkness. Lights had always swallowed the haze. That night in 1939, the lights of this world city went out for the first time. For protection from bombers. I froze in the sultriness, in the new night darkness. I felt the disaster, the inevitable end.

A cross hung in the sky to my left against a hazy full moon. The cross stood atop the Gedächtnisskirche (Memorial Church), its structure absorbed by the haze. I'll never forget that cross, its blackness against the haze.

Lines of cars down on the boulevard floated along like black, oily water, they too without lights for the first time . . .

"They will come and the entire Kurfürstendamm will burn and disappear," said a voice behind me. It was the voice of a well-known lawyer.

Two years later, he was arrested, convicted, and beheaded on the same day. He had helped many Jews across the border.

I wore a white dress that evening—and I felt cold. We went inside, closed the doors and windows and turned on the lights. I had already blackened out all windows with cardboard.

That night I experienced my first alarm. I didn't tremble then. We went down to the cellar, but not long. The all-clear signal came soon. Later there was a thunderstorm and cries for help from the street mixed with the constant rattling of trains in and out of Savignyplatz Station. Locomotives dared to whistle as if nothing had changed. Well, now they are going to the front, I thought and sleeplessly awaited the morning.

That is the way it began. What we anticipated came true. The whole street burned and lies in ruins.

Midnight

I must continue writing.

Opposite my former apartment, the state theatre is still

standing but shut down. Its facade too has partly crumbled. The building is somewhat intact. My theatre, I used to call it, had played there for months without pause, many wonderful roles. My favorite in that theatre asked me to play four different women, a housewife in the first act, a sophisticated wealthy lady in the second, a much too easy girl in the third, and a mother in the fourth. That play ran for two years. There were flowers and laughter, and the Kurfürstendamm was full of lights and promise. We could get real coffee, cocktails and fine liqueurs.

Today they sell red water. It's very expensive and induces nausea after a few sips.

Back then, all the shop windows were filled with things of fine quality, for babies beautiful jackets, bonnets and, yes, carriages. Ruins and worthless things of cardboard remain.

At the end of the day, I went to the coffee shop of my theatre to see Paula. It had been a splendid theatre café and is still open but now in the cellar.

We embraced. Paula manages as well as she can, serving corn-coffee, cabbage soup and ersatz beer. Paula is one of the few to whom I can still talk.

I started to whisper off to the side. She motioned not to. Microphones are everywhere in public places. She will come to Kladow to meet my son, and even offered to help me clean our little house. Domestic help has long been prohibited. All women aged fifteen to fifty-five must work in factories.

I asked for Vigantol in at least five pharmacies but didn't get any. Carrots! Two bags full. Then home as fast as I could. The alarm was faster than I. The siren started at the gangway on our side of the lake, and I hurried through the woods to my little boy.

31

What will become of the Big City? I fear to think about that, but the thoughts won't stop.

6

Eggs and Soap

January 28, 1945

We got special rations today. Two eggs! After seven weeks.

I cracked the eggs into our new pan and set the table for a gourmet breakfast. But the eggs sputtered in the pan, and the pan sputtered along with them. It couldn't take it, and the enamel finish burst into many little splinters, so tiny and sharp I could not pick them out. I had to throw it all away. My stomach growled.

In the afternoon, my baby slept in the sun at the back of the house. I wanted to clean up in peace. I shook the dust cloth out the window as an airplane came at us as if out of the field, quite low and terribly loud, right over our roof. It slid over the treetops and then a terrible noise, flames, smoke and so close, so close . . . could not tell if it crashed or dropped a bomb.

How quickly I ran down to get my baby.

January 29, 1945

Good morning, little boy! You slept through until 7:30, and I thank you. Your blanket again covers your nose, and hoarfrost, like sparkling sugar, covers the world.

Yesterday evening we had a surprise visitor. An old friend of Papa found us and brought a gift for you. Soap, real soap. Rationed soap is made of sand. He had buried this soap long ago. We talked freely. So good.

Now something that brings joy to us both, your porridge. How you cried the first two times, you expecting the soft rubber nipple and got only a hard spoon. Your fidgety little hands pushed away the spoon and spilled your precious porridge all over. But now we can do it so well. I set you on a mountain of pillows, hold your hands and you happily accept the spoon with porridge.

Oh, yes, something else. A stranger in a soldier uniform showed up at the door to collect clothes. "Rags shall be made of dinner jackets, dresses and coats," they had announced on the radio. "One should give everything away for the *Volksopfer* (peoples' offering). Only this way will we win the war." I had to find something to give him.

Now it is afternoon, and if Georg sleeps long enough, and if there isn't any alarm, I'll write about events not far back and always on my mind.

7

When Our Son Came to Me

He arrived with a crooked nose and a bulge on his head like a little hat. He lay next to me with purple bands and bright red mouth, his red tongue licking his lips. Love overwhelmed me, absorbed by the sight of my beautiful baby.

If he had waited six more weeks, he wouldn't have had the little hat or the crooked nose. But the bombers made such a racket and the guns shot so loudly that he arrived too soon.

Now his nose is nice and straight and sticks up. When Papa was here, he always wanted to gently massage it. The hat has disappeared too.

Soon after my son arrived, I wrote in my pocketbook calendar, "No words can describe the feeling when the little son lies in one's arms immediately after his birth, when he opens his eyes and looks . . . when the mother perceives in that tiny, somewhat crushed face his being, unfolding and wondering, the whole new world of his very own. *Der Sinn ist eingekehrt* (The Mind has entered). Now, only a few steps away lies part of my heart. And when you, little son, should land at the far end of the earth, our divided heart will always unite us."

It was nine o'clock in the morning on a Wednesday. A hospital vehicle drove me through the forest with Schwester Else as an escort. The sun squinted through the November fog, and the forest glowed.

We stopped at the house, large and grey. Babbling nurses scurried up and down a huge staircase. I sat on a bench and waited. Then, a strange door opened, and I entered. It was the *Kreissaal*, a new word to me, meaning crisis hall. It's the maternity ward and sometime delivery room. Right away the alarm sounded.

I waited in this room from Wednesday until Friday afternoon for the birth of my child. My whole system had cramped up from the alarms, from my fears, from weakness and spare food.

Then ultimate pain, life at its highest peak, the mask and chloroform a useless farce.

The sight: A man in white held a purple something upside down, spanked it, then silence, tension, at its peak, its gruesome grandeur.

The sounds: Sudden sounds. The infinite cry. The cry of the newborn. Life. Life! A voice: "It's a boy. A boy!"

The ultimate in joy. Overwhelming tenderness. Warmth. A baby! And it is mine, all mine, and it is a son.

He was tiny, just over four pounds and the basket in which the nurse put him smaller than the others. She tied a little chain around his neck and carried the basket to another hall with other babies.

Another air-raid alarm sounded that evening, and all the new mothers lay on wooden bunks in the cellar. The nurses brought twenty babies and tied them onto one mattress like spoons in an *etui*. I felt my son was not among them. Then a nurse brought him, and my heart melted, and I cried a bit. He in his little basket with a hot water bottle, and I was happy that he was by himself. He was so tiny and shivering.

The anti-aircraft guns shot, and the cellar shuddered. But nothing would happen to us. I felt sure of that.

The first trial came at five in the morning when seven babies were brought into our hall to their seven mothers to be breast fed.

Only I, the eighth mother, was again separated from my child. But I heard him, screaming and screaming. And oh, how I could recognize him! None of the twenty newborn babies screamed like he did, and it echoed through all the halls. But he had to wait till all his contemporaries were returned, and not until then was he fed with a bottle. I silently cried.

At the next feeding time, the young nurse brought him with the others, laid him into my arms, and I could try to feed him at my breast. But I had nothing to give him, no matter how hard we tried.

After that first time, they allowed me to give him the bottle.

I could not see enough of him to be at peace. The nurse assured me that the crooked nose would straighten itself out, and in only a short time the bump on his head would disappear. His tiny slanted eyes were almost always closed. Only once did he open them for a few seconds and at once closed them again with an expression as if say, "Oh, God. What is this that I stepped into?"

The Blonde Woman

In the bed on my left lay a young blonde woman. I smiled at her and wanted to say how happy I was, but her eyes were cold, cutting.

37

She had a very special baby. Every morning, a little before the seven other babies were brought to be fed, the head nurse appeared in person. She cheerfully held the baby high over her head, waved it and called loudly, "*Die Standarte kommt! Die Standarte kommt*!" ("The flag is coming! The flag coming.") And she laid that baby at the breast of the Blonde.

"What is '*Die Standartenführer*' supposed to mean?" asked the young mother on my right.

"That's the child of a *Standartenfürer* (Colonel of the SS)," someone said.

I became curious about this blonde woman, who I witnessed in her most human hours.

She devoured the political section of the "Volkischen Beobachter" (Peoples' Observer), a newspaper not seen anymore. She shook her head and read aloud with ad-libs, "Very good. Absolutely correct." She twitched her mouth or laughed as she read, and the same at radio reports. All day the torturesome radio blared into my peaceful heart.

On the fourth day, the Blonde got up and noisily rushed out to the waiting room. She beamed when she came back and spoke to me for the first time. "My husband has just returned! With his car from the Tchechei (Czechoslovakia)." She lingered on the word "car." An automobile is as hard to get as peace. All cars had been seized years before for use of high Nazis and the military.

"He brought me a present for the birth of his son." Back in bed again, she solemnly unwrapped the package and showed me ... A REVOLVER! She held it up high. "A Russian revolver," she screamed, and looked at it as if it were her newborn.

I turned away and pulled my blanket over my head.

Over these days as our little sons and daughters became used to their existence, gained weight gram by gram and grew more handsome, I learned more about the Blonde on my left.

Suddenly she showed me a picture of her seven-year-old daughter. "When we were abroad." She stressed "abroad" with a puckered mouth.

"Where?"

"In Holland."

I drew her out with short responses—really? Alas. Such as? Certainly—and learned more.

"My husband owns a castle, fifty rooms . . . he had four dogs . . . He always had guests and many stag parties. I wasn't there too often. I lived with my daughter in a villa in another section. We regularly went to his shooting range."

"What?"

"Yes, my little one is very talented. My husband taught both of us. I hit the bulls-eye every time. My little one can't do it yet."

Why do I listen? But then she continues.

"My little one goes right up to men on the street and says, 'You are Jew.'"

So that's how it is. The lordly brute murders innocent people in Holland. People like my baby and me.

And the Blonde next to me? His creature? Poor creature . . .

Then, there he was, in person. *Der Herr Standartenführer.*

It was the next day, in the afternoon. He sat at her bedside, depressed and morose as if under a tremendous burden. Did only I see this? No one paid much attention, not the nurses, the doctor. He wore his uniform coat with many colored and glittering decorations, but none of the mothers cared to notice him either, this executioner of Holland in the House of The New Born.

Other Mothers Near Me

"My husband is German-Romanian," the mother on my right whispers. "An artist. Acrobat. He is famous. He travelled throughout the world for fifteen years. Now he often says, 'I must have been crazy to come back home when the war started just because I was born here.'"

She showed me his photograph. A good face.

"People at home don't appreciate his loyalty in any way. Oh, what we go through. Gestapo! Trials! No work. He is not allowed to perform, and he couldn't even get work as an interpreter though he speaks other languages fluently. He is suspected because he has been abroad so long. If I hadn't earned money? But that hurts him more than anything. He now turns a lathe in a munitions factory."

Oh, the Gestapo, Hitler's Secret Service. Once under the Gestapo's watch, you are never safe.

The pretty young mother in the bed opposite me always seems happy. Every day she told us how terribly happy she was about her baby. And hers was truly exceptional, born with a tooth that pricked her at feeding time.

We heard her story.

"We come from America," she said as if not realizing what she had said. "Yes, I worked in a skyscraper." The word skyscraper always impressed people in Europe, and we all listened.

"I worked as a salesgirl in a department store. That was the skyscraper. My husband and I were born in Germany; that's why we came home at the outbreak of the war."

Someone asked if she had an automobile.

"Of course. A car and a nice home. My man is an engineer and had a good job. We had some savings too. But currency exchange wasn't possible. So, we put all our savings into clothes. Oh, we bought the most beautiful things, coats, furs, suits, dresses, shoes. We bought the best. We were taken care of with a wardrobe for the rest of our lives."

And the end of this story? The day after tomorrow when this new mother is released, she and her baby will move into a small room rented to her by strangers—without a husband, without dollars or clothes, without safety or a car. Because between her security in America and the happiness of her baby lies a long road.

The departing of a soldier: Her husband is far away on the front.

A bomb attack: Her home here burned down with all their clothes.

The road home to the Reich.

———————

I've been chatting and writing the time away. Outside it is silently and secretly snowing, and Georg is still asleep, and a whole day's work must be done.

8

Surprise Visitors and Silent Goodbyes

January 31, 1945

Paula was here and helped. Our tiny house is spotless now. I decorated our castle with pine twigs from the forest. Paula, such good companion, but twice we had to hurry down to the cellar.

All day the radio talks of the *Machtübername* (Hitler's seizure of power) over the last twelve years. When my son is a grown man, something will be said about this. Dear God, let it come to that, that then we will be able to talk, talk—and live.

Two in The Afternoon

It is over now, and baby sleeps, and our little hut is still standing.

I had just looked out the window when I saw them coming! Hundreds and hundreds of silvery birds with white tails glittering in the sun and all flying directly at our house. Weird. There was no alarm. I flew into baby's room, grabbed him bedding and all, and down into the cellar. During a pause, I ran upstairs to get the carriage and necessities. Roaring all the time. I saw two, three bombers crash not far from us. Many anti-aircraft installations sit near us.

Berlin was heavily bombed. The sun disappeared, and a black wall thrust itself up from East to West. Hours later burned paper and soot fell from the sky—out here 80 kilometers from the city.

It's getting more and more difficult to steal time. The alarm sounded at four in the morning, at noon, and now again in the evening.

But the joy with mine continues. For the last tags of his clothes ration card he got two play pants. My little gentleman's first trousers. A neighbor brought them from the city, and we were so happy.

I padded the hood of the carriage with pink silk. This bit of glamour originated in an old house gown I bought in Paris long ago. Today "Paris" sounds like a lost dream.

February 2, 1945

Speeches and more speeches on the radio. "Strong hearts! Nerves of iron! Victory." Then in between news about horrible circumstances in Bengal, India. Who here cares about India, about Bengal? It makes me sick. Then Ribbentrop, our foreign minister, said, "Our people are bomb safe." He should have to live here and flee to our cellar.

Directly under our window down on the meadow, sixteen-year-old boys in uniform train for the war, for the battle out here. They throw themselves to the ground, get up, throw themselves down, get up again and shoot live ammunition.

All the while, rabbits nibble in their boxes in our garden. They belong to a neighbor—not yet desperate enough to slaughter them.

February 3, 1945

Little boy, my dearest, what is all this coming to? I imagine us fleeing. But you know nothing of it. Your thighs are getting little folds, your cheeks a rosy hue. When I sing your song, composed only for you, you are as quiet as a mouse.

The Russians have reached Ost Preussen (East Prussia), the Oder near Küstrin. They have surround Posen and probably also Königsberg.

Papa's brother, Bruno the priest, and his sister, Maria, live there. Where are they now? Fifty thousand refugees from the east have arrived in Potsdam. Express trains are no longer running in our area. Since yesterday buses have stopped running.

Whatever I do is mixed with silent goodbyes. Mail has been restricted to postcards only. Gas has been locked off. Electric stoves, hotplates have been sealed. A man came, searched and sealed with wire and plug. Same with mailboxes.

Will we be able to keep our little home, our few belongings?

There was a terrible air raid today. I don't want to write about it anymore. There's a battle in Breslau—in the middle of Germany.

It is late now, but still February 3. A birthday today. Georg is a quarter of a year old. A silvery moon sickle hangs in the sky, wrapping all in its glitter. The snow, little houses, the bad airplanes, my husband, who too might be looking up there right now.

I almost forgot. Last Sunday our minister came and baptized our son. I draped myself in my most beautiful garment. It fit much too loosely.

February 5, 1945

Five o'clock in the morning.

If I only could perform real magic! I must prepare breakfast for five and don't know how. I don't have anything. As soon as the store opens, I'll speed to the grocer and persuade him to give me something, anything, in advance for our food ration stamps.

I hope he has something. Besides, all our laundry, all our sheets, are soaking in the big kettle in the laundry room to be boiled. I'll make a wood fire under it. At the same time, I'll get warm water for my baby's overdue bath. I don't know what to do first.

In the middle of the night a bundle of dark figures suddenly stood outside our door. Four refugees from East Prussia, our Uncle Bruno, Aunt Maria, and two of their friends.

My prayer now: That Georg sleeps for hours longer. Last night he couldn't, too much commotion.

February 7, 1945

Oh, how tiresome this is, all of us were in the cellar. When we came back up, our windows were broken. Dust and mortar lay around, the big mirror in fragments on the floor. It's not even ours. And baby was just greedily gulping his pudding when the alarm hit. Two bombs so close. I took baby as he was, half naked, and ran and pressed myself with him against the wall.

Later in the cellar, we huddled ourselves into a corner. More bombs. He screamed. I talked to him quietly, and gradually he calmed down. Once we even laughed a little together. But in my thoughts, I cursed.

I cursed the one who is the cause of all this insanity.

The Russians are marching in a wide front on Berlin.

February 8, 1945

I didn't have time to record how the six of us managed to settle in our two rooms.

The night they arrived, I went around to neighbors begging for blankets and pillows.

The same night, Aunt Maria began to play with Georg tickling him. She wouldn't stop, and he needed his sleep so badly. She is a spinster and doesn't know better. She doesn't know that babies are not to be played with. We, Uncle and I, both scolded her.

The refugees talk about their city in East Prussia, how it had to be cleared out in half an hour, that it happened so fast and unexpectedly. It had to be cleared out because what the Russians did not destroy, they plundered, raped, and murdered. In that half hour, one could get everything from the stores—clothes and meat and butter and canned goods.

But no one bought anything. Everyone rushed to get out of the city, get away before the Russians came in. Someone who had just killed a pig threw chunks of meat to the tide of fleeing people from his carriage riding out of town. Even we here now have something of this give-away, and it is good to be able to eat until one has had enough. Since the arrival of the refugees, we grown-ups have lived from these gifts.

Uncle Bruno left his parish, his roots, his life and work for more than twenty years. The big house and church lay behind, desolate, awaiting Russian occupiers or destruction.

And they tell us of the flight.

There in the east it is even colder, far below zero. These four were part of thousands, carrying bundles and children, carts and wheelbarrows streaming over frozen lakes and rivers, wading through snow sometimes as deep as a person. Many had to throw bundles and all their belongings away, fingers too frozen to hold them. Some sat on the road in the snow with feet too frozen to walk. It seemed more babies died on this flight than made it, they said. Our uncle buried two of them at the roadside. It hadn't been long since he had baptized both.

He paces back and forth, back and forth. He holds his Bible and prays. He often looks at my son.

I met him for the first time the other night at our door.

February 9, 1945

In the other room, Georg is crying a little, but sweetly and sadly.

I have just turned the light off and whispered a prayer. Yes, he is probably crying because he had to take his eyes off his little flowers. Colorful flowers on material which stretched along the bars of his little bed. He discovered them a few days ago. He looks at them all the time, turns his little head towards them, waves at them with both arms, and laughs and laughs at them. I must stretch the same material on the other side of the bed, else he will become one-sided.

Out here and everywhere in Berlin, they are building tank traps and barricades with the rubble of the bombed-out buildings. The trees on our main street have deep wounds. They have all been sawed to cut down easily and make ready for barricades. When I went to the drugstore through the woods, a soldier, holding two hand grenades, stood there in a freshly-dug ditch. How often did I travel this same path to go swimming, unburdened and lighthearted?

The Russians are fighting around Frankfurt an Der Oder, which is one hour from Berlin. I used to sometimes say, "When the Russians are in Frankfurt, we will be forced to surrender." Oh, were I right.

February 15, 1945

The refugees have left with bags and baggage.

And we? Oh, my little boy, I am happy and grateful for every hour we are allowed to remain here where I can cherish and protect you. Sometimes I have a silent hope that the war will be over before the Russians get here. Perhaps this little place on earth will be spared? Apprehensions and hope, side by side. The moments of joy with my son make me rich because everything around us is so terrible and poor.

But thoughts shove in constantly, of fleeing, of the possibilities for shelter nearby in the forest.

Now there is talk of paratroopers, the inevitable famine, of the great battle, right out here . . . then fear for my son's life, fear of cold, where to cook his soup? My thoughts circle around and around. Warmth. Take the most important things only. The carriage. No, the little bed also. The carriage will soon be too small . . .

Things to eat must come along, Mondamin, powdered milk, carrots, bottles, two, three . . . sugar is important. The grater for our carrots. No one will give me anything on the road because no one will have anything . . . Diapers, sheets . . . but where to boil them? In the forest? In an abandoned house? Matches!

Oh, dear God, the battle for Berlin may last for weeks. How long did it take in Budapest? Months.

I must get to the city. Try to get a ride somehow. Will look for Mr. Becker, my former superintendent. He has connections . . . He's among the few who haven't lost their minds. I will talk to him. He may know of transportation, perhaps to Bavaria, to my sister in the mountains? "We don't have alarms here," she wrote a while back. I must try.

9

Deciding to Flee

February 16, 1945

Haven't written a word for three days. Neither of my son's little world, nor of my evil, big world.

Yes, he is well. A rosy hue now appears on his little cheeks. His face is becoming charming. And today, for the first time, he smiled at me as if he recognized me. For several days he has been shouting mightily as if he enjoys shouting. And listening to music. Completely still. Whether the radio or me humming a song.

Today after his bath, as I dressed him on his wobbly table next to the green stove, he directed a fountain stream right into the middle of his bath water in the tub on the stool. I laughed.

It is evening, 7:30. My heart begs for no alarm. A candle is flickering sadly. We still have two candle stumps. And when they are done? Electricity shuts off at different times every day.

The Russians have *Die Schlesischen Kohlenfelder* (Silesian coalfields), the Americans the fields by Aix-La Chapelle. Chemnitz, Dresden, Kottbus bombed. One thousand five hundred planes, noon, evening, night. The radio announces only, "Achtung, achtung…

first wave ... second formation ... third wave ... fourth air attack ... from the South to the West, from Vienna to Graz ..." These radio messages accompany the passing of the day whether I am feeding baby, washing diapers, whatever I do. In the cellar three times.

There is a ring around my heart. It contracts more and more. I am deathly afraid for Papa, no sign, nothing.

February 17, 1945

Sat in front of the magic box and listened to the right frequency even though it is always jammed. First, I locked the apartment door and then draped a blanket over myself and the radio.

Well then, Churchill, Roosevelt and Stalin met in Yalta in the Crimea. They sent the world their plans: "We are determined to utterly destroy Nazi Germany. We are determined to secure permanent peace and prosperity for the world. We are determined to finally exterminate German militarisms."

Now I am waiting for current for baby's meal. Yes, I have hidden the hot-plate.

February 18, 1945

The uncle who brought us real soap called. I ran to the police station across the street. One can only telephone there most times, even though we still have a phone. He said that he lost everything in an attack eight days ago, house and store. A mutual friend was killed by the bombs.

Aunt Maria visited us. Some truck, acquired through their church, took her along. All four of them found shelter in a rectory in Nauen, an hour from Berlin. They received a permit for a shirt. That was all. No dress, no shoes, nothing. Cooking pots, she tells us, can only be procured by groups of twelve.

But the war crushes on, until there will be one pot for a hundred. Why is no one doing anything? Can't write any longer. There is no more paper, no notebooks. Can get a new notebook only in exchange for an old one.

February 20, 1945

The woman who lent us the little bathtub secretly sold me two notebooks. So, I can write again. Must write very small and abbreviate much.

Now to the most urgent thing. Yesterday I got an unexpected ride to the city to see Mr. Becker. He promised to help, and I gave him Dad's radio in exchange. He who today still has a truck, the necessary fuel, and a license is a king. Trains run only over short sections. Rails have been torn up by bombs.

I searched for Vigantol in vain. For carrots, a few. Went back to the theatre cafeteria. They have arrested Paula. She has already been sentenced to seven years in prison. They found satirical poems she had written about the Führer. That's why I waited for her all on Monday, also in vain. One must bear all this.

"*Wer über geweisse Dinge den Verstand nicht verliert, der hat keinen zu verlieren.*" (He who doesn't lose his mind over certain things, he has none to lose.) How often did I speak that line on the stage? How often do I think it now? From the part of Countess Orsina in *Emilia Galotti* by Lessing.

Near here is an underground shelter to where we now must rush at the alarms. There I kneel on the ground in the mud and spread my leather coat over us. The laundry room seems so insecure.

Is it possible that those who have brought all this upon us were once also tiny and helpless?

Outside it is still snowing, and the sun hangs in the sky behind the snow, a bright flaming disk. Every blade of grass glistens in its coat of ice. A beautiful world. No, this world they can't destroy.

February 21, 1945

A waiter in Paula's cafeteria has been executed, and a few weeks ago a friend of ours, a famous cartoonist. He too had a young son. His comic strip was called "Father and Son." Everyone looked forward to it each week. The "father" had a seal's beard, and the "son" was terribly curious and peculiar. Yes, and this father, the artist, said what many think, and now he is dead, and his son is alone.

I must quickly hang up the diapers in the attic before it gets dark.

Baby and I were in the forest today. Everything around us sparkled. A magical day, and my heart ached, and spring is very much in the air. I like so much driving my baby around in his carriage.

February 23, 1945

My dear little consoling one . . . That was all I wrote this morning.

Now it is late evening. Our Papa was here! The front is so near. We talked about everything for afterwards. A specific address here, another one in Bavaria, and of course his brother's address in Nauen. I made him promise to be sensible, to do the right thing. We decided we must leave at the first chance.

Vati und Mutti (Daddy and Mommy) stood at the window. Down in the carriage a sleeping face and all around many soft spring snowflakes.

February 25, 1945

The light is on now, and I can clean out and begin to pack. We need everything. Leaving something behind means losing it (although I hope that our boxes in the cellar survive). Drank the last of my coffee ration. At Christmas we received fifty grams.

Straightened out the desk and found theatre photos of parts I played. Will there be a theatre again? Found critiques, letters, a book—an address book from Berlin.

10

Entries in an Address Book

I opened to the letter D. Nothing is as it was.

Frank D.

Industrialist, Colonel in World War I.

Where might he be? I saw him last in 1937, during the loathsome summer days. Exactly at five o'clock one morning throughout all of Germany, *Die Volkswut erwachte* (The people's wrath awoke), a phrase exclaimed in headlines and on the radio over and over. Awoke and destroyed!

It struck at all non-Aryan stores. It smashed display windows, wrecked whatever was in them, threw furs and jewels into streets. Naked manikins lay on sidewalks like corpses. It splashed ink onto rolls of silk, threw precious material into the mud, struck at pianos and violins with axes. *Die Volkswut*! I wanted to crawl off and hide in shame.

A few days before that, I met Frank D. at Hotel Eden in Berlin. He seemed depressed but refused to talk about it. He said I shouldn't call him, nor would he call me and that he couldn't tell me why. He had favored the arts of Berlin with his power and his purse. He said he would leave that night for Switzerland and intended to be back in four days or sooner. We agreed to meet again at the Eden in four days at the five o'clock tea.

At that time, I played a part in a motion picture at a studio in a suburb of Berlin.

I saw Frank D. one more time, but not in Berlin, not in the Hotel Eden for tea.

One usually didn't have time to just visit, to socialize. But the next evening after seeing Frank D., I looked in on some friends who had stayed normal, who helped get passports, and helped their Jewish friends find a way over the border, any border.

When I got there, they whispered and nodded and dared not talk out loud. One of them mentioned names of wealthy Jews now on the list. On the list to be summoned by the Gestapo, never to return. I heard Frank D.'s name.

"It's better not to call," he had said, and his mood, the short visit, the flight to Switzerland all fit. But he did not seem to know he must never come back.

And now, what to do? I had to warn him. But how? It was late in the evening. But if he was already on his way back? No sleep that night.

The next day in the studio during dress fittings, I got my chance, one free hour. I hurried into the city to see his male secretary, whom I knew he trusted. As soon as I saw the secretary, I felt I could talk. In a low voice I asked him to walk with me to a particular store. The office might have already been bugged. A phone or telegram would be useless or deadly for us all. His secretary was sure Frank D.

would be back in three days now, had not taken much, had not made any plans to leave, to flee, to collect his family.

Frank D.'s secretary could not go. With the boss on the Gestapo's list, he might never get to board the train. Nor could any of Frank's family take the chance to leave by train for Switzerland. I had to go.

My only free day from shooting was the next day and the only means of travel to Switzerland the Night-Express. If I took the Express that night and returned with the same train, I would make it.

His secretary promised to get tickets and meet me at the station. He innocuously alerted Frank D. in coded language by phone about a business meeting in the hotel lobby the next morning. I was lucky. I got a taxi back to the studio despite restricted petrol to learn that my scene had been delayed for later that day or tomorrow. But to when I did not know. What if this scene, the most important in the picture, had been delayed until tomorrow? I had to get on the train that night.

We filmed my part of the scene just before seven in the evening and just before the shooting deadline for the day. The train was to leave at eight. Under my period costume, I was already dressed for the trip. I would take off my costume in the taxi and wipe off my make-up with cream and tissues already in my purse. I had to be back there on the set the day after tomorrow. It was my second motion picture, but I played like an old routineist.

And I made it.

On the return trip, before they let me on the train, they interrogated and searched me, even my little picture, a Rembrandt print of Christ, which always accompanied me. They picked it off the frame. But I made it. At seven o'clock that morning I stood under the lamps at the studio.

I had shaken the hand of Luck.

Frank D.'s telephone number doesn't exist any longer. The Gestapo have confiscated his house and business, but they couldn't take him in.

Anton D.

Actor.

He was outstanding as Mephisto in Goethe's *Faust*, unsurpassed as Miller in Schiller's *Cabale and Love*.

While starring in a play in Prague, he met his future wife. It was in the first year of the war, and soon they married, and at once he became acquainted with the Gestapo. They put him through judicial examinations, accusations and a time in prison, all because a German married a girl from another country. For a time he was able to stay out of the Army for continuous work in motion pictures. Hitler promoted the arts, the German arts. They finally took him at the beginning of this year. He works at an anti-aircraft site.

Nina, his wife, came to our little house on a visit and read from his letter. "My bed is a straw mat in the barracks with thirty-six other recruits. My uniform is old, too short and much too tight . . . Almost all of us are sick . . . coughing all night. Of course, there is no heat. Our drill instructor is twenty-five years younger than me. Now, our little apartment appears like a palace . . . Your rolls have not yet arrived, are they still coming? Need them badly."

Nina tells me of Anton's sister. She married a high official in armament and supply for the Nazis. Her telling reminds me of the butcher from Holland. "She lives protected from bombs and hunger in a mansion in the country. Her husband always wears his decorations, lots of them. She is surrounded by treasures we haven't seen in years. At the plum harvest out in the country around them, tons remained on the trees, rotting."

Nina puts a handful of this precious fruit on my table and talked on, "I quickly filled my bag. I hastily counted jars of her preserves . . . five hundred at least. Then she showed me rubies from Paris, beautifully set. I imagine the story of this jewelry. Anton should never know I visited her. He is angry with his sister since this marriage to that high Nazi and rejects any help from her. Right now, a corps of OT engineers is building a special bunker for all who live in the mansion."

OT stands for "Organisation Todt", Hitler's engineering corps. Many drafted civilians work for the OT in consummate slavery.

Nina wants to return home to her family in Prague, but she is afraid she'll find locked doors at home because of her marriage to a German.

Erich D.

Writer.

His screenplays were true to life, too true to life. He told colleagues, "It makes no difference if we make films for Churchill or Stalin. Our pictures must become art again. That is essential."

Last summer they sentenced him to death. A magazine expounded on his case for five pages as an example of "Criminal Motives of an Intellectual."

Alexandra D.

Ballerina.

She, beautiful and a great artist, was the ballet master of the Berlin Opera.

Not long ago at some meager vegetable stand in Berlin, we recognized each other. We stood in line staring, not sure. Fear, hunger, and tears have wiped away our beauty. At last we called each other's names at the same time, squeezed hands secretly.

She walked me to the bus. Trying to hold back her tears she clung to my arm and whispered, "I can't go on. I can't go on. One time I stayed home. A single day. Immediately the factory doctor looked in on me. You are quite well and healthy, he declared. What does he know? I'll go insane! Up at five every day. Cold. Almost two hours ride to the factory. At the machine from seven in the morning till five in the afternoon. Treading and treading, for ten hours! My feet, my feet. What my feet used to do and now can't do this."

She held her foot, very swollen. She still held her foot and she still cried when my bus pulled up.

Hanna D.

Costume Designer.

We, Hanna and I, once walked along the sunlit Champs-Élysées, high-spirited and laughing.

Not long before my son arrived I visited her, a thin, tired woman and a pale little boy with big frightened eyes. Her husband has fallen, and she has become a bunker-person. We walked to her bunker. On the way, she stressed how lucky she was to have that spot.

There it stood, a huge, grey cement mass without windows, perhaps five stories high.

We sat on her bed in the bunker. Her narrow cement cell is overcrowded with luggage, three bunkbeds, and over each bed a shelf. Four women and three children live in this aboveground grave cell. Hanna and her boy have spent every night in that small bed for a year now. After a time, I felt suffocated. The few air holes are no larger than the palm of my hand.

I glanced at the shelf, overloaded to the bursting point. Bottles and bottles. Milk bottles. Some bread. Medicine. Then I saw a glossy photo. "I know this, don't I?" I was not sure from where or when.

"Yes," Hanna said. "It's you."

I did not recognize myself in it right away. Too much has changed, and I have changed too much. That photo came from my first motion picture, also Hanna's first assignment as a costume designer.

Later, before I left, she filled my bag with two cabbages and a few onions. "Something from the garden of a relative," she said. A great surprise and a most valuable gift from my old friend, who now lives in a cell in a giant bunker—if she and her boy still live.

Marga D.

Teacher.

On Klopstockstrasse? Nothing stands on that street any more. The whole street has burned down. Only arches and chimneys stick up. I know nothing more of Marga D.

11

On Call to Leave

February 26, 1945

Terribly exhausting war-gymnastics. Up, down, up, down. Three times today.

Our carriage is getting heavier and heavier. I am losing strength and must pack more and more into it, never knowing what might be left when we come up. Our nearest bunker, the shrapnel bunker out in the field, has become so muddy that we again wound up in our cellar laundry-room shelter.

My "magic box" still gives me some courage. I turn it to the right frequency often. Though it is very much disturbed, I learn how far they have advanced. Then after days, our German reports admit some of it. It can't last much longer.

Hurriedly wash diapers by candlelight before the next alarm.

February 27, 1945

Last night my dear little son had his first nightly adventure.

At one in the morning, I heard the young gentleman chatting, shouting for joy. I opened the door, and there he lay in bright light, wide awake with the blanket kicked off. He talked to the little flowers on the drapes around his Betti, laughed at them, waved at them. It was my fault. When the current was locked off, I had put him to bed by candlelight and forgot to turn off the switch.

March 1, 1945

Down on the black, wet earth, sprinkled with grey snowflakes, a deer nibbles at the winter seed some farmer bent on staying has put out. God is still good. In the morning, I look out at a deer instead of ruins.

March 2, 1945

Becker called, got a message to me through a clerk at the police station, and I should call back right away. He answered. From now on we should be ready and prepared on two hours' notice. The truck may leave any day.

And baby? He has a bad cold. Worries. Everything is closing in.

Suddenly, today at noon, our landlady stood in front of me. With her key she came in like a ghost. I didn't recognize her, her face marked by war. "We have been living in the cellar for days," she said. "Our town is going to be completely destroyed by Russian artillery."

With three tightly-packed sacks over her shoulders, she fled back to her little house here. She hardly had time for a cup of corn-coffee, then had to make her way east again to fetch her children and her sick father. They will all move into this apartment with her deathly sick father. He has tuberculosis. We must be out, gone, when they get here.

I didn't ask why she must take our spot and not the apartment downstairs. She owns the whole house and can choose whatever she wants. Perhaps the man downstairs is indeed a Nazi big shot or holds something else over her.

Agonizing worries over my son.

Later

One alarm relieves another. Electricity and gas completely off. Only an arm full of wood for our one stove, for warmth, is left.

Baby's life continues, his little smile, his sweet sounds. We will get rid of this cold too.

One thousand three hundred bombers attacked Berlin. That can't be right, but perhaps it is. The sky is black again. I think there is not one city in all of Germany which wasn't bombed today.

Our hallway is filled with suitcases, the tub with diapers, the kitchen with dishes, and the room both boxes and crates. A few are in the cellar already. I had so much trouble nailing these monster boxes shut. At first, I didn't know how. Now it's going rather well. I hope they last until, maybe, the day I can come back here.

My demand in these demanding times: I must take the trunk with our most necessary clothes, suitcases with tablecloths, linen, blankets. Also, baby's bed, his carriage, boxes and bags with precious food, carrots, potatoes, sugar. But most of all his many cans of Eledon (dry buttermilk), which I have been collecting for a long time. A special formula, it's his life-saver. "Only if I can manage to load all this will we go," I said to Becker.

Down there in the backyard an old man breaks up the soil in his little garden for spring planting. How soon will tanks cross these gardens? Farther on in our lovely Scots Pine forest, war is expected. No flat spot left. All uprooted, slit-trenches, hide-outs and tank-ditches everywhere.

But in our laundry shelter one hears phrases such as, "Today, the army communiqué was very positive ... We certainly will win the war ... We must be victorious." *Will* and *must* are said as if commands.

March 3, 1945

Georg is four months old!

Dear little boy, stay alive for me. He still sniffles and sneezes loudly and strongly. They all laughed in the cellar when his mighty sneeze burst out of the carriage. Such a big sound could not come out of such a small carriage.

March 9, 1945

For a week now, we have been on call. Finally, a phone call when the phones were not locked off. "This afternoon at five o'clock will be the last fixed date," said Becker.

We stood on the highway where the truck was to pass, waiting and waiting. After two hours we went back home.

In the evening, a clerk came from the police station to fetch me. Becker called there when he could not get me. All anthracite coal was confiscated overnight, and the generator of this truck could not be heated by wood and so could not run.

Baby sleeps next to me in his father's bed. His Betti stands folded up in a shed with all our suitcases and bags. The old man who broke up our backyard soil for his garden helped lug our things. The shed is close to the highway at the point of our departure. If a bomb hits it in the meantime?

Here everything looks dreary. The curtain, the beautiful green curtain, has been taken down. The desk looks naked, shelves and walls empty. Thank God that the landlady has not yet returned.

"But there will be a truck tomorrow," said Becker. This one is an OT truck and is heading for Bavaria. He said he knows the driver and will do his very best. But if all our things can be loaded, he was not as sure.

I told him the driver can have my radio and a new pair of boots. Becker already has Papa's radio.

Part II

Running
in Hell

Katharina as Aimée
in Heinz Coubier's comedy
Aimée or Common Sense

12

The OT Truck

March 16, 1945

Yes, we are on the road. Haven't written anything in eight days. Will catch up much as my fatigue permits. I write this in a Red Cross barracks near Jena in *Thüringen* (Thuringia).

My baby is asleep despite kitchen noise and chatting nurses, despite the clattering spoons of greedily gulping soldiers, despite cold and draft, despite the damned radio and the creaking barracks door, which slams shut and open, shut and open in the wind.

And I? I cough, am cold and so troubled.

Where will we land? My sister in Bayern (Bavaria) expects us to find her, but here, in Thüringen, we don't know a soul. It is said that the driver got orders to go no farther than Stutzhaus, a small village near where we have stopped. Who shall take us in? My boy's little hands are hot. He perspires, coughs. We are both ill. Nevertheless, I must record . . .

It was already twilight in Berlin when we stood on the highway again. As the truck approached, I counted sixteen people sitting or standing among towering boxes. Sixteen items of unapproved, prohibited freight cramped in among approved war freight. And now the truck was to take two more items of prohibited freight.

We could ride in front next to the driver. Baby in my arms wrapped in blankets, so squashed I had to lift him at every shifting of the gears. When the driver and the others saw me standing there with carriage surrounded by wardrobe-trunk, suitcases, boxes and bags, they struck one clamorous chord: impossible.

They all looked at "the baby," and the baby smiled at them. Quickly, they did everything to crowd our load onto the overloaded vehicle.

On our right sat an Italian, the alternate driver, who made himself thin for us. When at last all our things were on the truck, the carriage stood on the street, forlorn, not a centimeter of space left. The only choice, snarled the driver, "Discard the carriage. Impossible." I wanted to cry. The Italian found some cord and carefully tied the heavily packed carriage onto the front fender and bumper. I will never forget him. I thank my son and his smile for getting us on that truck and the Italian for stowing all our baggage.

As we drove, tiny blue mittens in the carriage worked their way loose and dangled on their strings in the wind. At a stop, the Italian secured these too, a fine gesture in a hard time. The head driver didn't like what his helper did for us. He said harshly, "Am I glad that I don't have a child in these times. That's all I need."

This is our second stop. Our first after leaving Berlin was at an inn for truck drivers on the Autobahn. It was one o'clock in the morning.

My dearest was so tired, dirty, hungry, and crooked from lying awkwardly for such a long time. Always will I remember his smile on this road as if he wanted to say, "Mommy, I will make it all right."

We crawled out of the truck into total darkness and a cold rain whipping our faces. I couldn't see the buildings, only sense them. Holding baby in my arms, I carried two bags, a coat, a pillow and blankets all at the same time, every vital necessity. Leaving something behind is too risky.

We scurried to the shadow of a house. Every minute in this weather can be Georg's death. Gradually, I made out many trucks under covers.

Someone shouted out of the darkness, "Lights out. Alarm. Lights out." I did not see any lights to put out.

From nowhere, the Italian stood in front of me and offered to watch over our things on the truck until I returned. I laid Georg on some bench in the inn, thinking that babies are the only thing that won't be stolen now, and ran back to the truck for more items I must not lose.

Inside the air was so thick with smoke I had to push through it. Among many refugees, I discovered two other babies in the smoky, crowded room. They all, like we two, had the great privilege to come along as "war materiel" on one of those trucks. How many radios, shoes, cigarettes, fabrics, and cans of food have the truck drivers accumulated? The worst time has its advantage.

There was a kitchen where I could get hot water, change and clean my son, warm the bottle and prepare a few more for the road. But where could any baby breathe and sleep in this awful air? I found the best place behind the revolving door, where the air seemed a bit better. There he slept in his carriage while I rested my head on a table. But never long. Every few minutes I got up and checked on the carriage, on my son. People looked up shaking their heads. Some might not have known what I checked on so often.

At five o'clock in the morning our war-journey continued.

Where are the baby-chamber, the wobbly table, the flower drapes, the peaceful meadow and woods out back? That first day was particularly hard.

———————————

The Red Cross barracks here is our second stop. The entire length of the road was marked by auto-corpses, cars and trucks destroyed by low-flying planes.

And now our truck has disappeared quite suddenly, and everyone is troubled. Some say it is quite uncertain if he will ever return. Others say he left to unload nearby. No one knows anything anymore. We have half our belongings on the truck. The driver told no one he was leaving.

At noon, low-flying planes buzzed all around the barracks. Other passengers from our truck came over to look at "the baby" and asked about him, about us. When they learned we don't know a soul in Stutzhaus, the truck's last stop, they said as one, "You can't go *there.*"

"No empty spot is left, never mind a room or a bed . . ."

"Besides, the OT has put up their headquarters in Stutzhaus . . . The highest officers have moved in . . ."

"Besides, it's all a prohibited area of the SS."

"You could go there only if you were the wife of an OT commander."

Their warnings, their sermons continued without end. No one

offered a helpful thought. I could not blame them, all too preoccupied with their own survival in these times.

Later

Oh, my baby-boy! We had a terrible attack. The strafing and bombing planes follow us.

Nurses and soldiers alike ran out into the forest. We two alone stayed in the empty barracks, ran to the farthest corner, and I pressed us against the slim chimney. The whining, roaring and shooting, so close, hurt my ears terribly. Soldiers remaining at the door threw themselves to the ground.

When it was all over, the nurses returned pale and trembling and talked of craters throughout the forest.

Our truck has returned. We will leave now—into the darkening blue.

13

Stutzhaus

March 18, 1945

We are in the clear for a few hours or even days, but one thing at a time.

When we left yesterday, after the attack, they made us get onto the back of the truck. Very bad, because of a steady cold wind. I already had him bundled so nicely for up front when the driver grumbled, "Get in back! Have to shift often from now on."

I unpacked and repacked, putting baby into the carriage again. All this outside on the road in a streaming rain. We had to leave right away, no time to go back to the barracks to warm up the bottle. But then the truck engine wouldn't start, and we waited for two hours. During that time, I asked the driver to let me go back to the barracks to warm the bottle. Each time he shouted, "No, don't go! The truck might start any minute. I'll leave you right here, if you're not on it."

Baby's hungry sobbing interrupted by coughing hurt so.

Late at night we arrived here in Stutzhaus. Most of our co-travelers got off before. The remaining few vanished quietly with all their belongings to their own objectives.

And we? Where to?

The driver stopped, motioned us to get off and put our things down in front of some strange house. Dim light shone from two windows through the damp fog. The driver said something of a "village inn," started up the engine, and drove away.

Quiet, the rain had stopped. We stood, enclosed in fog and the faint scent of fir trees. I wondered that the lights in the windows were not blacked out. There must not be alarms here, and they must keep the electricity running.

I lifted the carriage up the steps and went into the house, into a lighted and warm beer room. Men sat contentedly at long wooden tables, heavy beer mugs in front of them. They leisurely chewed cigars.

It had to be Saturday, and these had to be the important town citizens, a small-town peaceful Saturday night, as if in another land far from any war.

I fell onto the nearest chair but could only sit for a minute. Georg was bathed in perspiration and so hungry.

They let me change and feed him in the kitchen. A heavyset woman, the innkeeper's wife, cleared an area on a kitchen table. I could warm his bottle and quickly prepared bottles for two more days. What did I know of tomorrow . . . ? Let there be a tomorrow.

The innkeeper's wife asked why we had to come here. She said, "The whole town doesn't have a spot left."

I asked her for a chair in the beer room for the night. I would have put the carriage up next to the chair.

"That won't do," she said with a snort and wave of her hand, as if she thought me an idiot.

My son happily gulped down his porridge and smiled again, a

tired, grateful smile. And I blessed my determination to bring along all his food and milk cans. I asked again if they would not perhaps . . .

"We can't help you," she said with more finality than before.

A good fairy sat in the shadows on a bench at the back of the kitchen for a late visit with the innkeeper's wife. She took us in.

That's where we are today. She lives on the second floor of the inn. I slept in a real bed. My son got real milk today, and he talks again and laughs. The kitchen table for his care is large, and I can cook his soups in peace.

Talk now, my son. Tell all the stories of this bad journey. Our Good Fairy with snow-white hair and red cheeks is listening too. She could be eighty or a hundred. Because today is Sunday, we are all in the "Good Room" (her living room), baby in his carriage and I am sitting and writing next to a large tile stove where logs crackle. The calm of the forest pervades the room, and a brook in front of the house gurgles.

Stutzhaus is deeply embedded in wooded hills in a valley, a town of perhaps five hundred. Our Good Fairy's name is Frau Klein. She is a widow, the owner of the tavern and the local brewery across from the inn. The brewery is shut down now.

March 19, 1945

Alarms blare out here too, but I no longer tremble so.

Georg twists his little face showing his scorn at the noise. He knows what can follow. His carriage is shrinking, and he can't stretch properly anymore. His beautiful Betti waits in some storeroom among OT material. I will ask Frau Klein if we may set it up, then find the mayor and ask permission to stay here in this prohibited SS area. A young lieutenant, who took up quarters at Frau Klein's, is to leave soon, and then we will get his room, she said.

On the radio: Berlin was heavily bombed yesterday with many other cities. The Americans are moving towards Mannheim and Frankfurt. The Russians have taken Neisse, Danzig and Gotenhafen. The net draws tighter.

March 20, 1945

Back from the Village Hall.

Remaining here? Impossible. Food ration stamps for two days only. It is true. The highest military headquarters will be set up right here.

Who, how, what? No one knows. Tunnels are being dug into the mountain rocks. I see everything from our window. Trucks unload cables, boards, bags of cement, tools, machinery. The Americans will laugh. Perhaps they can make good use of these tunnels.

Autos with SS officers come and go, all still running on petrol. For many weeks now, the SS officers have been arriving with truckloads of furniture, have moved into houses and apartments, all cleared by force.

"Two villagers have been shot because they objected," whispers Frau Klein.

March 22, 1945

I visited the mayor's place, and he saw me.

I said, "My husband is an important OT engineer and follows us. I expect him any moment."

He didn't say more and did not ask. He let me register to receive food stamps. Now we can stay. A guardian angel must have stood next to me.

When I left, his secretary, who sat in the other room, glanced at me as if to say, "We know . . . we are with you . . . We think as you do." I don't know how she knew what I think and that my husband is no OT engineer. Perhaps because I'm not a factory worker, and my baby is still alive, the mayor thought I told the truth.

Surprised and happy, I went on my way.

March 27, 1945

Georg lies exhausted in his narrow carriage, his eyes dim and feverish. His little face is beautiful even in pain. It started last night with complaining and moaning, sounds I never heard from him. A temperature of 41 degrees (105 Fahrenheit). His throat is covered by red spots and his mouth is swollen. He takes Fenchel (fennel) tea, but it does not help.

Above us the planes flew so low that the diapers on the line over the kitchen stove trembled. They came between two and four at night. I knelt by his carriage and prayed that he would pull through. Frau Klein stayed in the cellar.

At eight in the morning, low-flying aircraft threatened again. I suppose they too know about the "highest military" moving in all around us, have been following our mad army from wherever it came here.

I had to run to the community nurse. She promised to see Georg in the afternoon and guessed his condition to be scarlet fever or measles. His temperature has gone down a little, but his body is covered with spots.

Afternoon

The nurse was here. It is German measles and a bad cold. Such tired eyes, no longer a smile, such complaints and coughing. And fever. The trip was too much, the disorder.

The nurse talked of all the babies who don't survive these treks. "Three little children died here in the last days," she said.

Yes, we need peace, but peace is nowhere.

The radio echoes through the apartment at what must be its highest volume, shouting out FINAL VICTORY. It talks of the Führer's greatness, of want and hunger in England. It calls back into history. They talked of Hannibal today.

March 25, 1945

The white carriage glistens in the spring sun. It already warms.

I am sitting on a tree stump, at my feet a dark green moss carpet cut by a crystal-clear spring, wrapped in fragrance and the tranquil tunes of the beautiful Thuringia Forest. Tall pines sway in the pure air of this famous forest. In times past, many found peace and new health here.

Georg continues to complain and is hot. This morning his pillow was wet. I thought he was sick to his stomach. While feeding him, I discovered pus flowed from both ears. That's why he screamed so when I touched his little head. Such a terrible grown-up sickness. All good spirits stood by and helped him.

We are waiting for our own little room, waiting for the lieutenant to leave. He is only twenty-two and commands sixty soldiers and thirty-five trucks. They can't leave because all roads have been bombed out, and they can't get fuel.

"Soon they'll be transferred to the railroad," says Frau Klein with a comforting smile.

He uses his time well, the young lieutenant, mostly by eating in

Frau Klein's kitchen. Every evening he noisily enters the kitchen carrying many food packages. Our Good Fairy fries, bakes, and steams on her wood-burning kitchen stove for the *Herrn Leutnant.*

She goes about every task for this man with much respect and talks of everything military with reverence. She admires that perfectly good man, Hitler. So, we have an overheated kitchen and the tantalizing aroma of almost forgotten food—eggs, bacon, steak, beans, cheese, and more.

The young man offers neither his landlady and cook, nor a seriously ill little boy, one bite. I am hungry and don't even have potatoes. I silently curse. Some of our collected potatoes were left behind in Kladow in my prince's old paradise.

But let us be grateful that we could stay in this village, that a fairy rescued us.

March 26, 1945

A good day. This morning one of the lieutenant's men brought our trunk and suitcases and the Betti from the OT storeroom. I still have some cigarettes from Papa's ration to barter. One cigarette is worth a lot.

March 28, 1945

The Americans are in Würzburg, about 160 kilometers away. If only our Papa were here, if we could be together. I gave a letter with the agreed-upon address to a soldier on his way to Berlin.

We went to see a doctor in the nearest town, Ohrdruf. I had to push the carriage through a terrible dust storm for two hours. We found a doctor and learned what is wrong. My son has an infection in both ears and suffers from malnutrition. He should be able to hold his head up. Instead it hangs and falls from one side to the other. The lack of vitamins, especially vitamin D and Vigantol, is very bad. He needs sun and more sun. The doctor talks of lemons, fruit, things no one can get. But we did find Cebion (a vitamin C preparation) in a nearby drugstore, also some calcium tablets.

We must catch up with baby's nutrition. How, I don't know. So, God help me.

Again two hours' walk back, with the carriage turned around so baby would not face the wind. I had to sit down at the side of the road for a while, exhausted.

March 29, 1945

We have begun already, caught sunlight. Baby is lying naked in the window under real sun beams. Just a few, but they will help him get well.

March 30, 1945

And today another soldier brought Vigantol, a great surprise. He bought it in a neighboring town, also for cigarettes.

I have been very troubled these last days, even while so close to peace and the end of this madness. But I'll get Georg healthy again. Now that a new world is coming, he must grow into it strong and beautiful. If Stutzhaus will be spared and not turn into a battlefield, everything will be all right.

Down on the street, they are coming and going—the strange, important men. Most are in uniform with heavy golden decorations, cold and arrogant faces. Their cars stop in front of the tunnel, they get out, look around, discuss intently, then leave. Our young lieutenant, with his sixty men on foot, can't move. No locomotive runs to take them away.

My son is very pale. One ear still suppurates. Now he gets calcium, Cebion, Vigantol, and his carrot juice daily. I brought the carrots from Berlin, and I clean and grate the dried-out carrots with much effort. Not many are left.

April 1, 1945

Today is Easter Sunday.

Pines rustle in the wind, sun, rain, thunder, fog. They take as it comes.

Our main purpose: Catching sun-rays, each day a little bundle of sunbeams on baby's right side, a little bundle on the left. He likes to lie on his stomach and is already starting to lift his head. He tumbles onto one side and laughs and laughs and chats again. Yes, we are over the hill. We'll make it. Another great improvement: His Betti has been set up in the living room. Our Good Fairy did that.

A morning farce: Each day at eight, the lieutenant has his men stand at attention in front of the house.

The war terrors follow us. Low-flying planes strike at Stutzhaus, their explosions everywhere. The main target is our tiny train station. The whole house trembled while baby lay in the sun at the window.

14

Grace in Horror

The Russians have taken Küstrin on the way to Berlin and are approaching *Wien* (Vienna). The Americans have taken Kassel and occupied Heidelberg. Undamaged, and I am glad. Heidelberg is a very lovely old city. Only a year ago, I lived there in a house above the *Neckartal*, a beautiful valley through which the Neckar River flows.

It was still rather peaceful then ...

Die knospenden Hügel schweigen

Und schauen den Frieden an

Ich gehe still meine Strasse

Und fange den Morgen an ...

(The budding hills are quiet/ and look at peace/ I walk my street in stillness/ and begin the morning)

That was the first stanza. I had quiet to absorb, to translate the charm of the valley into verse. Every night I played in the theatre. Then came "Monika." For this part, I traveled to Düsseldorf. I must write about it.

May 7, 1944

Only a year ago now, all theatres that could function were still open despite hunger, confusion, and bombs—a command from above to help boost the people's morale. Air raids would often interrupt our performances. Actors and audience rushed into the theatre basement-shelter, and afterwards everyone would come back and the play finish.

Sometimes we could not finish, and we heard of nights when no one would come back up.

Yes, only a year ago there was an "Opening Night," a new play, and a guest actress in the lead role. The play was written for and dedicated to me, an honor every actress cherishes.

Düsseldorf, once a most beautiful city, was called The Garden City. Its streets were named after flowers and adorned by many blooms with fountains in their midst. Happy laughter filled the outside air, as well as its fine stores, excellent hotels, and Rhine wineries. The "Gay City," it was called too.

The flowers are gone, covered by grey rubble and sand. Hotels and shops burned out. Air raids for over a year have done that. "There will be an alarm every night," I was warned before I left home in Heidelberg. "But sometimes there are three or four."

As the train pulled to its stop in the city, I stared at the bombed-out station, wondered if mine might be the last train, if I might see my home again. A guest house close to the theatre had saved a room for me. It was one of the few remaining open guest houses in the city.

Soon I saw the playwright and director. Someone placed flowers in my arms. I didn't like these flowers, so out of place. Acting in this theatre was out of place too, but I had to see this through.

The rehearsals began. The playwright looked pale, lacked the usual excitement for his play's opening. He had come from the front, on leave for this honor. "On the front, you can fight back," he said.

I already knew what air raids had done to the State Theatre of Mannheim, where I was under contract. Mannheim had been leveled and our theatre there destroyed. We next played in Schwetzingen, a village close by Heidelberg. There, we found an old renaissance theatre building. It had hand-carved seats of gold backs and yellow gold seat cushions. Its railings were gold too, the whole theatre like a giant gold and yellow jewelry box. In the eighteenth century, the Count of Schwetzingen sponsored that theatre. No air raids and bombing runs had yet struck Schwetzingen.

Here in Düsseldorf, the air raid alarms sounded every night, but in my first days of rehearsals only a few bombs hit near.

At my dress rehearsal, I found gorgeous, heavy silk, soft velvet in bright colors waiting to choose for my costumes. "The famous *Düsseldorfer Schauspielhaus* depository is still complete, amazing," I thought and hoped it a good omen.

And then, suddenly, it was May 7 and our opening night. My stage fright, as usual, and despite the horrible real world, enthusiasm for the play, for the part.

When the curtain rose, I was a young lady in love on my way to see my fiancé after a long time of waiting and worrying. He too was a soldier, though in another war. In the play, he and I had only a few hours and even these arranged with great caution and concealment.

As soon as the curtain dropped on Act Two, sirens screamed. We all (actors in costume and audience) silently made our way into the basement-shelter as fast as we could. It had high arched ceilings, safer than modern buildings, and I welcomed it.

We actors huddled in a dark niche. Bits of the audience's low conversation, their first-hand critiques, reached our ears.

"*Sie is jung, sehr jung . . .*" (She is young, very young.)

"*Nein, Ich wises, dass Sie schon 30 Jahre alt ist.*" (No, I know she is already thirty.)

"*. . . Sehr gut . . . die Liebesscene war herrlich.*" (Very good . . . The love scene was magnificent.)

"*Ich weiss, das Sie verheirated ist. Sie ist mit . . .*" (I know she is married. She is with . . .")

"*. . . Das ist sein bestes Stück.*" (That is his best piece.)

Any great tragedy numbs. Great wars numb everyone caught in them. In their numbness, those who have no control, no defense, grasp for normal things. This audience here in Düsseldorf must have been theatre people grasping at one more performance. They didn't talk of alarms, only of the play and the actors. Soon we heard the all-clear signal and started Act Three.

Spontaneous applause broke out in that last act and at the play's end. It was a success. No one lingered. Everybody rushed away to be home by the next air raid.

That next air raid came on us a little after midnight. I was awoken by sirens and collected my things, always in reach. I slipped into my heavy leather coat. It had protected me in many shelters, and I covered my head with a scarf. There wasn't time to dress. I reached for my purse, my bags with a warm dress, underwear, shoes, a blanket, a towel, soap and toothbrush, a bottle of water and my food ration (half a loaf of black bread, pound of margarine, quarter pound of sugar and dry milk), some incidentals worth saving: papers and letters, "The Hands" by Rodin, an ivory Madonna, both cherished gifts.

The guest house was blacked-out. A small staircase led to its cellar, soon crowded. It was narrow, damp and dark save for a single candle.

We guests had hardly settled when the house and earth started to shake. One loud explosion followed the other—interrupted only by the whistling of bombs. Not now, not on this night. I had to live, my insides screamed.

I began to pray aloud. Other voices joined, all of us praying to the tunes of the inferno outside. At a strong shake, our one candle went out.

Two hours before I had been wrapped in silk and happily talked of love. I had bowed to applause . . .

Nothing was left but a prayer in the dark. I searched my purse for matches. I knew I had some but couldn't find them. No one had a flashlight, no batteries available for a long time.

An explosion hit close. A rain of mortar fell on cheeks and hands. Someone whimpered. I again searched for matches in my purse. I felt the envelope with Papa's letter. I held it tight. I heard his words, *"Sei tapfer."* (Be brave.) *"Es soll Dir nichts geschehen."* (Nothing shall happen to you.)

Still alive . . . still alive . . . The explosions stopped. Perhaps there was hope? Hope is the last thing . . . that can face immense evil.

We waited, listened. All was quiet.

"Es ist fünf Uhr," (It is five o'clock) someone said.

We moved slowly, carefully out of the darkness towards some light, grayish and faint. The wooden staircase hung like a darker streak. We crawled over heaps of rubble and broken glass. Someone held onto the staircase and each helped the other up to the main floor. The front door was gone, a dark, smoky hole.

I went outside—cautiously. It was hot outside. A strong wind blew. Glowing cinders fell onto my coat. I crossed the street to a park. Trees and all were covered by ashes, flames everywhere, an inferno of burning buildings in many places. A city in flames. Low detonations but far away.

I sat at the edge of some fountain, warm water still in its basin. I soaked my scarf, hung it over my hair, and looked back to the street, to my guest house.

The entire street was gone, all of it, but for that guest house. It stood like a chimney on a burned-down property, narrow and tall without windows, with cracks in the walls, but there it stood. Whole. All the houses on this stretch were built abutting the next, so this had to be a miracle.

I stared.

Beautiful tunes drifted in, and I wondered if I had gone mad, if my hearing had failed me. I looked around. In all this chaos, singing? I stood up, dazed. I walked toward the tunes, over to some bushes not burned to ground. Nightingales among the ash-covered bushes sang the morning in.

I wept.

Part III

Combat
Too Close

Undated photo of Katharina
on the last page of her
Scrapbook, Volume 2.

15

Death's Three Divisions

April 1, 1945, late in the evening

Massive changes have descended on our little village, with rattling and clattering since two in the afternoon. I look down to the street from our window in the "good room." War's precursors have arrived. The peaceful burbling of our little brook no longer reaches us.

Vehicles upon vehicles push into the center—wagons, vans, trucks, small convertibles, huge oversized armored cars the likes of which I have not seen. Green tree branches cover most of them. From the top, large trees hide a tiny car. It is as though the forest itself were moving. But the branches can't hide what lies below, all the vehicles heavily dented, some smashed, but they chug and lurch along. I wonder what battles they have seen. After the lighter vehicles, tanks, tanks upon tanks rattle through Stutzhaus.

Soldiers walk with the vehicles or hang onto every open spot. Every fender seems taken. Other soldiers ride in on bicycles. Are they still soldiers, these men without caps, without coats or bags, without sword belts, guns, or rifles? They carry cardboard boxes under their arms. Strings around their waists hold up trousers, their uniforms ripped and faded, their faces grey patches.

Those on foot support themselves on sticks made from branches, and all of those who walk, every single one, limps. I look again. I can't fathom it, but it is so. Not one among them walks with a normal gait. A procession of cripples. Their approach from every direction feels like Death creeping in.

At precisely this moment, the radio shouts from the kitchen, shouts of *SIEG!* (Victory) and compares Hitler to Caesar.

I mustn't stay at the window. My dearest will have a bath, a cherished enterprise. Water is on the stove, and our Good Fairy somehow found a large basin.

All my thoughts, all my worries boil down to one: Will my baby survive the near future, the looming carnage?

April 2, 1945

It is four in the morning.

The rattling has continued all night, our house shaking all night and still shaking. I had to see. I threw on my wrapper, took notebook and pencil and went to the good room's window.

Down there more masses are approaching. Out of the twilight, out of the forest-gloom towards our house, masses of soldiers, masses of vehicles. Divisions? It must be divisions. Don't know how many men there are in a division. I'll ask.

Down there on our little bridge over the brook, almost in touchable closeness, a tall soldier, bearded, dirty, tattered, gesticulates with a wooden stick like a conductor. He directs the divisions through the village. His trousers have the red stripes of a general. He too limps when he walks up to vehicles to direct them. Stamped by defeat, is all I can think.

They approach without pause . . . Will our tiny wooden bridge hold under this burden? Where will all these men and material stay, form up, fight? How?

Noon

The ground, the air still rattle and rumble. Yes, I've learned three divisions are moving through our town.

When I got milk this morning, the country parson came into the store and told us that only one division had moved through, that two more are expected and that the general took up headquarters at his parish. Everyone here worries.

Your bath, your soup, your dear life all continue—for now.

The lieutenant left suddenly. The general ordered him and his well-rested detachment to scram. They had been here for half a year, doing nothing except eating and acting the big shots.

We two were able to move into the *Kammer* (small unheated room) he vacated. I cleaned and rearranged to create a space for the Betti. I glued a few little pictures onto the wall. It's too small for a chair, but it's our own little castle. If we can keep this with our belongings, if we can keep our heads up, if we can find our Papa again, then, yes then, we will pull great Good Fortune out of this war.

I went downstairs to the beer room to call the doctor in Ohrdruf. No connection. The room and hallway are packed with soldiers. Shreds of their conversation:

"Five hundred deserted . . ."

"Two hundred vanished . . . foolish."

"Senseless madness."

"Dive bombers all around us . . . what for?"

The innkeeper's wife says, "Every bed, every cot, every nook has been vacated for staff officers . . ."

How long will they let us keep ours?

April 5, 1945

War has descended on our town. Carriage, baby, and I are deep in the forest. "Houses will be targets only," many said. We are hidden in the fold of deep moist moss. I camouflaged the carriage with a green blanket. It is quite cool, but my baby is still warm and snug. Low-flying planes circle all around us. From afar, the trickle of machine guns.

I write this in my notebook on a tree stump. I must. So tired.

Yesterday, Frau Klein walked with us into the woods. Today she couldn't make it. She is almost eighty. Yesterday we stayed here for a long, long time in rain and snow and storm.

Today we rushed up this hill to our hiding place. Under air attack. The planes search for divisions here in the forest.

Will our fold of moss protect us? It is hidden in dense fir trees, not far off a path. No one can see us, but I can glance out and around us.

I took three heavy bags, clothes, bottles, cans, my bread ration. In my rush, the carriage got stuck in the mud. I hope it's still there on our way back.

Now, I'll give him the bottle. It's still warm.

Scattered deserters crash through the woods near us.

An old peasant wagon, drawn by two tired white horses, rattles along the path. A clutch of soldiers hobbles behind it, deflated, heads down. Their commander, walking beside the wagon, tries to reach them with a hoarse, despondent voice, "As long as there is the slightest chance. I'll break through. We'll fight... can't say it's senseless, let's go home..."

I wrote it down as heard it. Even as I wrote this down, two in his small unit deserted, fell away and hid among trees.

The wagon rattles on through the forest, packed with a regiment's meager remains, a few machine guns and cardboard boxes.

Other deserters keep limping by, uniforms and shoes in shreds, their faces desolate and hungry. Then, soldiers with that alert, quick look, with that "we'll fight until victory" look, they too pass by, but not many.

A portly woman leading a blind man up the hill shouts at them: "Why don't you throw that down?" pointing at the grenades in their hands. "Why don't you stop? How long are you going to take part in that shit? You stupid fools."

There, suddenly, in front of me stood a soldier. Holding onto a branch, he almost fell into our hollow. I knew that he had long ago thrown down his weapon. He is starving. He asked emphatically, too empathetically, "To where does this path lead?"

I directed him to our inn. The innkeeper's wife, if she is there, will give him something to eat, show him the secret way through the forest, as she has with others...

I rummaged through our bags for bread, but he was gone.

Evening

Chilled through and through we are home now, and our carriage sat unharmed where we had left it. Georg has been cared for and is at peace. But I must record.

16

In the Center

Fleeing started two days ago on April 3rd. At five o'clock in the afternoon, all high-ranking SS Führers and their families scrammed head over heels, with goods and furniture, packed all their belongings into their still petrol-burning automobiles and trucks and drove off. They left panic behind. Many civilians still here began to scream, to pack, to run.

The inn's waitress packed up and ran. Two years before, she had fled with her two boys from air raids in Düsseldorf to the quiet here in Stutzhaus. Her room is above Frau Klein's apartment. While packing and rushing, she babbled and warned of the horrors to come but didn't say where she planned to spend the night, the next day, the next week.

She left late in the evening with many others in an old horse-drawn wagon. It creaked in all its joints under the heavy load.

No one wants to be in the center of a battle. Rumors circulated. People shouted. American tanks, many tanks, had made it to Ohrdruf, eighteen kilometers from here. They have occupied

Meingen, Eisenach, Gotha, fifteen kilometers away.

"They'll pulverize every house," people screamed.

"Murder . . . hanging . . . rape," drip out of distorted faces. Our radio propaganda has worked as intended by Goebbels.

Soon the battle front would be here. In an hour? That night? The next day?

Everyone lugged suitcases, boxes, bags, chairs, and blankets into the village's rock cave-shelter farther up on the main street. It's built into the mountain and secure. But we did not go there, not a spot left. Long ago the tiniest space had been assigned to Stutzhaus citizens. That morning I saw a thick white cloud billowing out of the entrance, and I asked if there was a fire.

"Oh, no. It's only the used-up air," they said.

That afternoon artillery bombardment had begun, creeping closer from one detonation to the next.

Lights and radio went out. The last radio reports were about our new food rations: one quarter pound of margarine for three weeks, three pounds of bread for three weeks, no meat, no flour, nothing else.

Later in the evening the artillery fire ended.

I dragged all our belongings, everything we have, into the cellar except for the heaviest trunk that I had managed to lug with us. I put my son to sleep in his carriage, stretched out on my bed, fully dressed. Ready.

There was some artillery fire during the night, but for a few hours it was quieter than any nighttime.

Yesterday, April 4th

In the morning, I ran for milk during a low-flying aircraft attack.

While waiting for my turn at the store, a boy came crashing in shouting, "They have left Ohrdruf! They have left Ohrdruf!"

They were almost here. What is eighteen kilometers for America?

When I ran home, I noticed milk in my pot. In all the panic, the good woman filled my pot.

Then everything at once. Packed my dearest into the carriage, packed bags, heated milk, filled three, four bottles, then rushed with carriage and all up the woodland hill to find a hiding place. Our dear, old Good Fairy hobbled along behind us.

We squeezed ourselves under the thickest fir trees. Baby's little face was covered by fir needles.

On the alert and tense without ceasing, we finally noticed the quiet. After long hours, chilled to the marrow of our bones, we went down the hill and home. There we got the news: The Americans altered their course and moved on to the north and south of our village.

"If they only would have come," I said over and over.

Last night artillery fire. Hard hits, bad, terrifyingly close. Uninterrupted shooting in the distance. Fire behind the hills. Horrible hits in the early morning. Strikes, at half hour intervals, grind heart, nerves and mind. The village inn is the biggest house in town. All the other houses are smaller and most spread through the valley.

The artillery fire stopped at nine this morning, April 5.

Now, as I write this, dive bombers are over us. I don't want to go down into the cellar again. It is damp and filled with rats. I shudder at the thought. And horrible air, so bad for him. Last night we were down there four times. The carriage is heavy, the staircase deep. But he was asleep in the carriage when I carried him up and down. We have one small candle left.

The situation: The Americans have occupied Ohrdruf and Arnstadt. We are in the middle, and with us the encircled German Divisions. But what is "us", a few hundred miserable civilians among three divisions, three generals, thousands of men? And they are all here in the village of Stutzhaus and hidden in the woods nearby. From here the Divisions intend to break through, to what, when?

Our mayor wants to surrender without a fight, but he has been overruled. Who is he against three divisions and three generals?

The last OT technicians who built defense structures and stayed behind are now demolishing all their newly-built works and frighten the villagers with many explosions. Tons of documents are burned and ripped to pieces. The most secret papers of Hitler's Third Reich turned into white shreds. Heaps of wet paper choke our brook and turn the clear water a murky grey.

In all this, we still breathe the fragrant, clean forest air. In all this, I must give my little boy a bath, as windows clatter at the roaring of bomber squadrons above.

Martin, fifteen-year-old Frau Klein's nephew, storms into the kitchen. He shows us spanking new boots. He looted them from a vehicle shot to pieces in the forest. "All the people go hunting in the woods for tossed away uniforms," he says.

I am so tired I could fall asleep on the kitchen table, in any chair, maybe standing like a horse. Against the roaring of planes, I struggle to stay awake. Dear Lord, protect us.

April 6, Afternoon

No milk anymore. Closed. I asked everyone I could and learned our next-door neighbor has a cow. I will go to him and beg for milk. I rushed to the baker for bread with our last food ration stamps. Got some.

It is cold and raining hard, patches of white fog over treetops on the hills. There is shooting in the forest. Evening approaches.

Soldiers. All of them are in our town, yet more are coming. Since early in the morning, they have been moving out of the forest back towards our inn. Swarms of them. Whispers say the soldiers gather here for the great counterattack. I can't bear to think of it. Now there is no fleeing into the forest for us. If we leave, we might never be able to come back. If we made it back, there'd be no place left in this house of Frau Klein. She could never stop the hordes of worn-out soldiers from swarming in here.

Late in the day

Yes, I really gave him a bath, despite it all. He is lying in his carriage, shouting for joy and babbling and babbling...

While outside, in front of our house and everywhere, grim war-monster tanks move around and around as if lost, driverless, but many men hang onto each one.

17

Layers of Madness

April 13, 1945

The war has roared over us with all its horror, peril, pain, and grandeur. Has shown its skulls, tried us to the fullest. Were I not so tired, I should shout for joy. Shout with you, my son, that we came through this.

We two may walk many roads, but that we managed these days of hell on earth we must thank God and shall never, never forget Him.

The present

It is six in the morning. I am sitting in the kitchen writing this on the kitchen table by precious candlelight. I found a few candles left by American soldiers in the inn's toilet.

My son is lying in his little bed. Yes, it is still whole. Frau Klein is deep asleep on the kitchen sofa, and I have just rolled up my bedding from the kitchen floor. All three of us slept here in the kitchen because...

In front of me are my notebook and bits of paper on which I

jotted down what happened to us in these infernal days. I will begin at:

April 7, 1945

Soldiers and more soldiers pressed into our village, singly and in throngs, worn out, hungry and sick.

A few piled into our cellar inflated, arrogant, clothed in shiny leather coats, saying, "*Der Führer*, latest weapons . . . *Endsieg* (Final victory)."

Their orations bolted up out of the cellar during artillery fire. American artillery aimed at us, at them. These idiots.

The inn was a beehive, inside and out. They loitered around the place, stood on the little bridge, groups of them, looking up at the reconnaissance planes, completely ignorant of the civilians' terror of planes. Low-flying aircraft whizzed around continuously.

Then—suddenly—it was upon us! Falling bombs! Shooting! I flew into Georg's room. He was asleep, soundly, and warmly huddled in his blankets.

More falling bombs, awfully close! I threw myself over his bed. *Shall I tear him out of the warmth into the cold cellar . . . it might be over before we can get out . . .*

A shot! Directly into the room! I pulled him up. Couldn't grab him properly. Got him. At any window it might hit us . . . How we got into that cellar I don't know. Squeezed into the farthest recess . . .

An avalanche. Shelling. Bomb hits. Whizzing of bullets. Explosions. All upon OUR HOUSE.

The staircase crammed, up to top step, with a mass of uniforms. More hits upon hits. Shrill. Hurtful. Baby screamed terribly.

I cried and shouted and screamed, "This swine! This Hitler!

This Bandit! Why doesn't he stop? These criminals, these murderers. Why doesn't anyone do anything?" More came out of me, out of my soul. It all had to come out.

Around me some two hundred soldiers, crowded as sardines, among them the big shots in their leather coats. *Now they will shoot me in all that misery . . .*

But no one moved.

After hours of quiet we dared to go upstairs.

In Frau Klein's good room neat bullet holes in the window. I studied our Betti. There, the distinct round bullet hits on the frame, on his pillow. Broken glass, dirt, and mortar all around. In the front of the house in the little brook, an unexploded bomb.

I feverishly collected urgent things, filled bottles and the carriage. Frau Klein was so distressed over her broken flowerpots, windows, the dirt everywhere. Immediately, she began to clean up. I thought to tell her it isn't over, that much worse is expected, but kept quiet.

We found some cardboard for the windows. At the slightest sounds of war, ever so far away, I packed my son into the carriage and lugged the overloaded thing down into the cellar. At least ten times that day and evening.

At dark, we went down for the night, down to the rats and mice. It was arched low, cold and damp and filled with the stench of rotten cabbage and old roots. I worked the carriage into a small space between cabbage and potato patches. Rats scraped and peeped around my feet all night.

The shooting receded but never stopped trickling in the distance. After one long silence, my wristwatch showed three in the morning. I carried Georg upstairs for fresh air.

Right then, everything shook. A hit, on our house. A tremendous explosion smashed into my innermost being. It knocked me down, but I managed to stagger up again, got my feet to work, could see and hear.

We flew down again. Frau Klein followed. She wanted so much to lie down for a while.

We decided to stay in the cellar until morning. I couldn't stand up anyway, not anymore. I fell onto a dirty board—tired unto death.

Suddenly Frau Klein stood over me. She held up a huge bottle, yellow liquid in the bottom. Whiskey? "Left by Herrn Leutnant," she said, smiling weakly and handing me the bottle. She's an angel. It was enough for a mouthful.

April 8, 1945

It was Sunday, one week after Easter.

All my life will I remember, will I thank you for how well you behaved in these days, that you are brave and patient. You often smiled at me, especially in the cellar, in all that atrocity, as if to say, "It's all right, Mommy . . . It will pass . . ."

Or during the nights when I carried you up and down, you slept through, through the shooting, the bodies and rats, through it all.

I lugged many of our things into the cellar, heaped them into some corner. All my furs, the leftovers from peace and the theatre. From then on, I draped them over the carriage for protection from the dampness, from mortar falling.

The divisions didn't leave, the soldiers stayed put, their numbers grew by the hour.

Our inn remained the dominant focal point. The pitiless headquarters of the generals and their staffs. Yes, they all moved into the inn, mostly into the cellar.

Everywhere lamentable predictions by the villagers: "They will shoot the whole town to bits if the soldiers don't leave . . ."

"I hate these generals . . ."

"What do they want without weapons, without bread?"

But the generals kept their abominable ambitions to the end. It was said they again wanted to force a breakthrough. Through what?

And outside it got awfully quiet all that day. No shot, not near or far?

And my husband? Strange. I hardly thought of him in these days. Too exhausted to care. My God.

A Potato Blessing

During one of the long lulls, our kitchen stove was covered by all the pots we had. Filled with potatoes boiling away. To feed the hungry soldiers. Down in the inn's kitchen the same. I could fill my empty stomach. I hadn't had potatoes for a long time. How often did I ask the innkeeper's wife to sell me a few? She always refused with a dry, "Haven't got any." But officers must have ordered all potatoes "upstairs" from the cellar and wherever else they lay hidden.

More new soldiers arrived, came walking, from great distances. From the east: Danzig, Königsberg. The south: Wien, München, from Schlesien, from every corner of the Third Reich. Did these soldiers belongs to anything? To a unit? Who thought about that? Who cares if they deserted? The only thing anyone knew was that they came walking from far away, that they now too assembled here with us.

Their talk, always the same sad melody.

"If only my wife . . ."

"If only my children . . ."

"If I can only find them again . . ."

"I have to find them . . . If I don't find them . . ."

"If only my wife . . ."

"If only my children . . . "

Connections are long lost, everywhere, with everyone.

Two men begged me for warm water and a bowl. "For our feet," they said. Their shoes hung in shreds, covered by bloody crusts.

"We have walked for eight days without a rest," they mumbled.

They sat on my bed and I cut off their shoes, washed their bleeding wounds. The baby oil served well. Diapers torn into strips became bandages.

I was able to help others. But then what? They could not stay; the war was not over. What can heal in a war? On the front? I could not think past the moment.

Stutzhaus became an ant-heap! Covered by soldiers. Streets, houses, walls, paths, smothering the village. And always a line of these grey ants strung in and out of the inn, in and out, endlessly.

I got help too. A major helped me carry our huge trunk down into the inn cellar. He is from Vienna, he told me, an opera singer. While shuffling the monster trunk down the stairs, he chanted in his opera voice, loudly and clearly for everyone to hear, how happy he is about the Allied victory, about the end of the Nazis.

He not only helped with the trunk but also presented me with a gift—his butter ration (about 60 grams). It was for the baby, he said. And for me a can of sardines. I hadn't seen butter in years. Sardines? Took me a while to get over it.

Some more good fortune. All morning we caught sunbeams. After that, I pushed the carriage across the street over to the brewery cellar. It was huge. Its heavy doors were open to the street. As soon as we got there, I saw a plane and pushed the carriage inside.

The cellar to the old brewery was immense, arched and filled with oversized beer barrels. Others also sunned themselves in front of that cellar. At the slightest sign of danger, we all ran inside. The sun is so good. While Frau Klein watched over Georg, I rushed to warm the bottle. No more porridge, but I gave him his pills and drops no matter where—in the woods, in the cellar, and here in the sun. My hands shook so badly I could not count the drops.

It was quiet on the front all that midday.

An old man talked to me. "Why don't you go with your baby to Ohrdruf?"

That town had been in American hands a few days. They surrendered without fighting. It's peaceful there now. We went there to the doctor. But the heavy artillery fire came from there.

"The American army is kind and cooperative," the old man said.

Yes, I thought then, tomorrow we will go. That thought kept me going.

Artillery fire all night, not exactly at our inn, but getting closer and closer.

April 9, 4:00 in the morning

I began to pack again. All our belongings, which I had hastily thrown into the cellar, were moist. I packed what I could into the trunk

All that night uninterrupted traffic, men, officers, everywhere. Moving and moving. On the staircase, in the inn, in the rooms, everywhere. Moving and moving, up and down, up and down. Even the generals came and left, came and left.

The innkeeper and his wife now slept in the cellar, bedded

under feather blankets, propped up on huge reclining chairs set in among the cellar cabbage piles.

Monday, April 9

Early in the morning.

I wanted to leave for Ohrdruf between eight and nine, the time without curfew, without shooting. Somehow, from somewhere people of the village had heard about curfew times from the Americans, a time when they promised not to shoot, not to dive bomb.

But I couldn't make it. Just too tired to think, didn't know where to begin. This is the front, but all we have, all our possessions are here in our chamber and in the cellar. If we take too much along, the carriage would break down. Anything we left behind had to be packed securely for afterwards.

But first bottles, baby-food cans, clothes, sheets, and whatnot. Too much to do right now, and too late to leave. We next had to go between two and four in the afternoon, the next time without curfew promised by the Americans. There would be no shooting then.

At noon I fed baby in the cellar and dressed him for the journey. Shooting and shooting and rumbling without let-up, quite close. I ran up and down and up and down and hadn't finished packing, when all Hell broke upon us once more.

Plunged into the cellar. Threw myself over the carriage, my leather coat over both of us, so his ears wouldn't be hurt. Hundreds of soldiers blundered into the cellar, many wounded on stretchers.

Shouting at the foot of the staircase. "Artillery fire, artillery fire! Right on our house," yelled soldiers around us.

The strikes repeated and repeated, ground nerves and senses.

"Will the cellar support us? Will the cellar hold us?" I asked the soldiers many times.

Again and again they assured me the old arched cellar is quite secure and will last.

So, War, come ahead, I thought. Too late to have left for Ohrdruf. Had I finished ten minutes earlier, I might have left ... and we would be dead.

April 9, Late Afternoon

I went upstairs with Frau Klein to get bottles I had put into hot water for our intended flight. She searched for an old kerosene burner to warm them in the cellar. We grabbed tools and blankets and hurried down again.

I changed my baby. He babbled and laughed. Yes, even during the artillery attack I heard his happy RRRRR sounds, his babbling. Thank you for these precious tunes, for this happy life in all this death.

Nine in the Evening

Soldiers brought food rations. Bread and cans of meat fat. The men formed a line and fetched their rations. They told us, "One general and many wounded men sit in the brewery cellar."

The supply officer hastily came around to us and hurled at each of us a loaf of bread and meat-fat. Then he scurried off.

Someone said, "He's running away through the forest. The Americans are already on Kienberg (Kien mountain)." This mountain frames the town.

If they had only arrived here. It would have stopped then. Despite the new food, I doubted I could go on much longer. I was terribly cold and exhausted. But Georg slept. If no big bombs dropped, as in the cities, I thought, then the cellar would last. Bombs were not supposed to be dropped on the front, too close to both sides. That's what the soldiers said.

Suddenly only a few soldiers huddled in our cellar. Had they gone? One by one and in groups, they fled into the forest on this night. No one stays to the end.

April 10, Four in the Morning

Very little shooting. The rats scratched and whistled. Wretchedness constricted my heart.

Frau Klein went upstairs to lie down. Was it courage, or nearness of the other world? She was on the threshold that makes us strong and indifferent or perhaps stupid.

Shooting started again but in the distance, knocking upstairs on the floor above the cellar. Tanks rumbled on the street. American tanks?

The innkeeper got up from his chair-bed, went upstairs to check on the knocking. He shuffled back and grumbled to his wife, "They want to blow up the bridge."

Want to blow up the bridge! His words tugged at my brain like an electric shock. Blow up the bridge? What now? Baby's lungs will burst from the pressure, the explosion. Water will flood in. We will drown. Where to in the middle of the night? During artillery fire? Oh, my God.

18

Sobbing for Americans

I asked the innkeeper. "Where? How? Who?"

He didn't answer, took the carbide lamp and left up the stairs with his wife. They left me alone, in the pitch-black cellar, alone with my baby.

I groped my way after the innkeeper.

A soldier stood in front of the door. I stared at him and could not bring forth one word, totally bewildered. It was dawn.

He grinned at me and said, "Yes, yes. Apparently, I am the last."

I grabbed his sleeve, begged him to help me, to accompany us to the cave, the mountain shelter, into which we didn't want to go until now, where only the good citizens of Stutzhaus had been allowed.

I packed up the carriage with bags and blankets, and, with some presence of mind, snatched up the kerosene burner, and the bottles. Otherwise I was spent.

This madness. Blowing up the bridge. Without any thought for the villagers. And this stupidity. The Americans conquered the Rhine, they won't conquer that little brook here? The senselessness shouted to the heavens.

For eight days the men and their generals, the trucks and tanks, had been fleeing from them. Precisely here in Stutzhaus, precisely now they wanted to defend.

I pushed the carriage through the hazy morning, under fire not yet right here, to the upper part of town, to the cave. That last soldier at the inn carried our bags.

A man stood at the entrance of the cave. He had an intelligent, friendly face. I went in. He assigned us a place and asked a woman to guide us. He showed me a white flag and said he expected the Americans any hour.

The Cave Itself

A heavy, stinking substance, the air inside, hit body and brain. Rock walls glistened greenish with water slowly sliding down to the ground, down to people, and more people, an ocean of faces. Spooky faces, pale green, sweaty, sorrowful. Carbide lamps sparingly illuminated this merciless scene. The sick lay in the mud on the ground. One of Dante's circles of hell.

On the path through this dreadful hollow no wider than one of my feet, we got bumped from all sides. The supervisor came to our aid, lifted the carriage and explained why we too needed a spot, and led us on. He told everyone that their two bridges would be blown up, the one by the inn and the other farther upstream. Lamenting in trembling voices, words of worry about homes near the bridges. We were hardly settled when sounds of close detonations rumbled through us, then more. How many family homes were flooded, broken, wiped away by these maniac generals?

Mud covered everything low in the cave. Baby sweated and steamed, and I stood in the muddy water up to my ankles. I couldn't clean his suppurating ears but managed to change his diaper.

I had to wind my way back through all this once more, through men, bundles and mud. Baby was starved. I had to warm a bottle. The kerosene burner and our other things were left at the entrance. "The only place where you can light the burners; too many gases inside," the supervisor had said.

Two meals had already been skipped, and the bottle didn't get warm. Low planes drove me back into the cave. Baby greedily drank it cold.

Everyone whispered how badly, how longingly they awaited the Americans and quiet, and peace. The words "peace" and "Americans" passed from mouth to mouth like a prayer.

I heard "Max" and "Max" again. Max was a French prisoner of war let out of our cave to approach the American lead tanks with a white flag, to implore them to preserve the cave. If I were alone, I too would have done that.

From the entrance came a rustling and rumbling. A man wound his way through to the middle of the cave. "The priest, the priest," came from every direction.

He stopped, and all was quiet. Tears running down his cheeks, he said, "The American tanks are going through our village."

Every man, every woman began to sob. Everyone. The sobbing echoed through the cave, a mighty chorus of sobbing. Every normal person had suffered so terribly under these Nazis.

My tears flowed. Free, of that madness, of bomb fright and all evil. Through my tears I said over and over, "Free, free."

To hold out. Minutes, hours? If I fainted in the bad air, there was no one for my son.

An old woman lay dying in the corner. Her bony, yellow face glistened in the carbide light. A blind man was led through. Anxiety overwhelmed. Everyone tried to push forward to the entrance, where the supervisor sent all back to their spots.

Two hours passed. Finally, an announcement: "Families whose homes are located next to the cave may leave now."

19

Looting Among Ruins

April 10, 1945

A woman offered to take us along. I don't know how she knew we lived down in the town and would have to stay in the cave hours longer. Her home is nearby on the mountain, she said.

It was high time my dearest got out into the clean air, got washed and fed. Our blankets, coats, everything was soaked and full of mud, and outside the sun shone.

At the house of the strange lady was a little fenced vegetable garden. I hung our things on the fence to dry. I washed Georg on a small kitchen table while at least fifty people came and went. They all washed up in the kitchen sink. I lay my baby naked on a clean diaper on a little patch of grass in the garden.

Down in the valley, perhaps a hundred meters below us, sits our war village. American soldiers and their tanks, guns, machine guns, cannons wait and watch us from their positions in the meadows up to the houses. "Are they to be used some more?" I whispered.

What did that concern my son? He kicked about happily naked in the warm sun and shouted for joy. He had had a good meal, a

Nestle Baby pudding from one of our precious cans. And an apple, a gift days ago from Frau Klein.

What might have happened to her? On the way out of the cave to here, I had advised the grumbling barkeeper that she had gone upstairs to lie down. I hoped she was all right . . .

And our inn, our little kingdom? It sat down in the valley, perhaps 500 meters from where we were. But I didn't dare move a step closer.

April 10, Later

Shooting started up again and grew heavier and heavier all around us, but it seemed to be aimed away from us, from the village. I hastily washed diapers and hung them up in the sun. Washed the carriage. Pillows, everything was soaked. The mattress in Georg's carriage was so soaked it could be rung out.

At night the strange woman, she is from Cologne, offered to share her bed with me. How happy we are to lie down. Before that, she even gave me a dish of warm soup, thin but so good.

The quiet didn't last long. The American heavy artillery sits on the top of this mountain over the house where we tried to recover. Without end they shot in the direction of Schwarzbach at the fleeing Reich soldiers. The whole mountain shook.

We two were again under my leather coat in another cellar, built into rocks, age-old and overcrowded. It was big enough for ten people. Roughly thirty squeezed in.

The shooting was bad, and my ears hurt. But we knew it was aimed away from us, and that the Reich soldiers could no longer shoot back.

Then the planes lay down blankets of bombs in the forest where all those Reich soldiers had fled to hide.

The battle of Stutzhaus, a small battle and one-sided, but too much for our senses and could have been avoided. So many communities surrendered peacefully.

Not until dawn could we leave this cellar.

April 11, Midday

All was quiet on our little front up the mountain.

I searched for Frau Klein, and for a new spot for us for the night. The house here with its little garden had become overrun by relatives of the strange lady from the big village cave.

I drove our carriage through the midst of the war's tumult, past guns, tanks, tents, troops, all enveloped by a thick cloud of dust, and pushed through to our village inn, our home in the town.

The inn was destroyed. I thought, one more puff and the rest will fall. Roof and its beams in pieces, the front gone, tatters of curtains flapped in the breeze, not in broken windows but on trees in the garden. The cellar appeared to have remained whole. In front of this ruin, American soldiers were rebuilding the bridge over the brook. It was almost finished. They appeared young, alert. All are slim, move fast, athletic.

We found Frau Klein across from the inn, at the house of her relatives. We embraced. She looked relieved to see us. This house remained intact.

But it held many people, also the town's mayor and American officers. The mayor signed a document renouncing Hitler. Some citizens of Stutzhaus received white armbands. The town's new police force had been formed.

Signs, placards were put up. A crier with a bell walked through the village. He cried out, "Between seven in the evening end seven in the morning no one may leave the house. Anyone on the streets will be shot, immediately."

Frau Klein's people took us in for the night. Some tenants on the second floor had a kerosene burner and let me cook my son's pudding. That night we could sleep in Aunt Clara's room. Aunt Clara is eighty and dying. "Any minute now might be the end," they said. Frau Klein slept there too. But I didn't put Georg into that death air, moved his carriage into the hall for the night. Here he caught another bad cold.

But I must write of yesterday in the mountain house, before all the relatives came and we had to leave, and before I found Frau Klein, of the day itself.

Yesterday, the many friends and relatives of the people who owned the mountain house reported, tearfully, of plunder and destruction.

"Oh, God . . . I no longer want to live." Many said that.

"Everything . . . my beautiful porcelain."

"The last eggs . . . for my cousin's jewelry . . . "

"The kitchen cabinet tossed over . . . "

"My husband's watch . . . "

"Suitcases broken open . . . "

The whimpering and crying continued for hours.

Yes, a kitchen cabinet can mean as much as warm sunshine on a new life.

Two American soldiers entered the house, unlocked and searched everything, but did their work fast, were polite, and left quickly.

I thought of our things in the inn's rat cellar, our most

important possessions—baby food that I had saved so carefully. Milk powder, oatmeal, cans of Nestle powder, all in the trunk in the cellar.

In the afternoon, Georg had a terrible adventure in his carriage in the sun in front of the mountain house. A scared rooster flew up onto his carriage. It still hopped around the carriage when I came out at my son's screaming. He trembled all over. I took him up into my arms and promised to not let him alone for a second.

Despite that, I had to leave and search in the inn's cellar. I pushed the carriage into the house. Frau Klein promised to watch over it until I returned.

I was the first civilian to enter the village inn over a narrow board, the bridge not yet passable. Rubble everywhere, countless artillery hits in the walls, the garden, the trees. I stepped over large branches wrenched away, lying among metal pieces from exploded shells. The staircase hung freely, but I could get up it.

Our little room. Miraculously, it seemed the least damaged of the entire house.

Das Gute Zimmer (the living room) did not exist, all destroyed, shattered, its furniture gone up in dust, gone, dissolved. In the middle of the floor sat a heap of rubble, chunks of wood, wire, plaster, and on top of this, almost untouched—Georg's little white bed! A good omen and new courage.

Then down into the inn's cellar.

Water up to the first step. I had to give myself a push and wade through to our luggage, dimly lit by a dormer window and, thank God, somewhat higher. Everything was broken open, strewn around. Oatmeal, honey, cans of Eledon milk, a shoe, all floated in the water.

I fished things out as fast as I could. My jewel cases were empty. Shoes, dresses, blouses, linen lay in the mud, everything ransacked and overturned.

With a feverish haste, I carried things up to our room. Yes, the room was virtually whole. Only the door was out of its hinges. I leaned it up. Took three hours to lug some of our stuff through the water and up. I found cord and fixed the hanging staircase as best I could for the time being.

While carrying the last heap out of the cellar, I found a dry loaf of bread and an open can of animal fat and plunged into them.

My son slept rosily and soundly during his mother's adventure. I got his bottle and a clean diaper but then had to go back there again.

Second time in the cellar, in the water again. I could hardly believe it. Someone again rummaged through our remaining things down there while I was gone just now.

I had all the remains upstairs just before seven and curfew.

Frau Klein came over to the inn's kitchen, it too in pretty good shape. Some crazy town woman came with her, harassing her, screamed in a shrill voice. "Now that everyone is let loose, you can't leave anything in this ruined house. If you do, you'll lose the last you have. Anyone can get in. Anyone."

Then both packed up what they could find of Frau Klein's possessions, from wooden spoons to gloves, and they too carried them to a safer place.

And I? How could I carry our things away? It was seven, and the curfew had begun. I just made it across the street to my son.

He lay in his carriage, awake and smiling at me. I told him about the little miracle of his white Betti and that soon he will be able to stretch out.

I made my way back into the strange room for the night, prepared the bottle and in the light of dusk boiled some spaghetti for me fished out of the water in the inn's cellar—and cried and cried . . .

Our Papa? Where is he now? Where is our home? Our home with him and nowhere else?

Deep sleep came over me in that room with dying Aunt Clara.

20

Picking Up, Picking Through

April 12, 1945

Georg has a cold.

We couldn't stay there with Frau Klein's relatives much longer. But perhaps we could move back to our little kingdom at Frau Klein's apartment when the stairway was supported, the blown-out windows covered with cardboard. All three of us planned to move back into our little kitchen and our room. We might be able to heat the place, because the kitchen stove was undamaged. Much to do.

Lucky again. An OT man crossed my path. He had been one of our co-passengers on the truck from Kladow to here. I offered him my last cigarettes, Papa's last cigarette ration, and he helped.

In a very short time he repaired so much so well that we were able to move back. Sturdy cardboard filled in the top part of the front door. It worked. Even the little bed got reinforced by good cardboard on the few remaining posts. That night my little boy could stretch out. Normalcy of a normal life began again.

Someone found a dead horse up the street, and we got whole armloads. We can quiet the hunger for days. We boiled it right away, so it won't spoil, and we could skim off the fat.

Eleven at Night

The first night in the patched-up home. I had heated a lot of water and was just about to wash in baby's tub on the floor by the light of a few candles, when someone came up the stairs to our door.

My heart beat. Then pounding on the door. The cardboard caved in like paper. Someone reached through and turned the key from the inside, and two figures crept into our kitchen, the baby bed in the center.

I, still standing in the dark behind the door to our little room, heard Frau Klein's voice. "*Was ist los? Wir haben ein Baby hier. Leise!*" (What's the matter? We have a baby here. Quiet.)

I thought they would go now at this sight: old woman and baby. But they went into the room next to the kitchen, once Frau Klein's bedroom. They moved about loudly, sure of themselves, with good flashlights. They approached our room. I got out front and faced them. Two Americans.

I blurted out English, better than I ever thought I could. They searched my bed, my closet. A slight smell of whiskey came with them. "We are looking for soldiers," they said.

One could have been about eighteen, a Hollywood Sonny Boy, I thought.

Standing there in front of the door I talked and talked into the blinding flashlights, at the two shadows behind. They got to hear my whole story. My marriage, my career, my fear of bombs, my troubles, while I sobbed the whole way through . . .

They gave me everything they could find in their pockets, chewing gum, cigarettes, matches, chocolate, shook my hand and disappeared down the stairs.

From then on, all three of us slept in the kitchen.

April 15, 1945

Constant coming and going in our broken house, a constant search for Third Reich soldiers at any time. The cardboard section of the front door caved in a few more times. Then I took it away altogether. Our OT man still hammered and nailed and glued.

Someone left behind a great curiosity in the inn's backyard garden—an entire radio station trailer. It's the center of attraction for many American soldiers. Each day while hanging diapers, I hear more of its story. It was built in France but has been hauled about for five years, from Salonika in Greece to Smolensk halfway to Moscow, to its end under shattered linden trees in our backyard.

Curious, I went inside to the shiny compartments, the precise wiring in many colors, this secret work of a scientific brain. Fascinating, even for me. But every day it gets further dismantled and plundered until not a single wire of any color is left, a skeleton Radio Station Trailer among diapers and shot-out trees.

The German Army also left behind a lot of sausage meat for its dogs, left it in the brewery kitchen. Frau Klein and I garnished it with salt and pepper and again boiled it to extract the fat. Thus, we got animal fat for many days, two pots full. And more lugging water from far away. Cleaning, washing, sorting, and forgetting.

The sun came out and shone all evil away.

Aunt Clara died today.

And my son? What does he care? He progresses in peace or war. Reaching out and grasping his milk bottle, recognizing Mom and things around him, indicating the need for his potty. For the very first time I could hold him back until we were over it. And talking,

talking and talking. Now he holds up his head, almost. While I feed him, he plays with everything in reach. He is also getting handsomer, and dearer and more loving and loveable. My dear Georg Johannes.

April 17, 1945

Fragrance and blossoms and flowers and fresh green branches fill the world. I place violets and cherry blossoms into the carriage next to a sweet sleeping face.

On our way to Ohrdruf to see the doctor, sharp cannon shots burst out. Three times the sounds went through and through me. Why? I thought. Then I remembered. They are for Roosevelt's funeral, the president of the United States.

Civilian radios don't work yet. I only hear things told from one to the next. Hitler is supposed to be in Japan. Goering dead. The Americans in Berlin.

Where is Papa?

Someone in our town is said to have an AKU (battery-powered radio). I will go there and ask if I may listen.

In Ohrdruf we got some carrots and turnips, at least a kilo. Nothing else available there, besides a little black bread and for one month two pounds of meat. We still have some cans of baby food, and the doctor was satisfied too. Things *are* picking up.

April 18, 1945

Our village thunders and vibrates under giant wheels. Yes, roaring monsters descend on Stutzhaus, this time all American war vehicles.

Trucks and tanks, far too many to count. On many of them German prisoners, packs of them like grey dusty bundles. Also women, *Blitzmädchen* (like WACS). One of these trucks carries a street sign at the front of the radiator: *Adolph Hitler Strasse.*

Tracks of war line every road and path. Heavily damaged single little houses, trampled fields, battered trees. But even in the tracks new green grass in coming up, bright green strips in the deeper tracks crisscross the open fields. This new green is the mightier force.

Everywhere, in the woods, by the railroad tracks, in gutters at the roadside, in the tiniest nook, lie glistening clean little boxes, little round cans—"for dinner", "lunch", "breakfast" cans tossed aside by the Americans. All of us rummage through them and often find coffee, cocoa, cheese.

April 19, 1945

The sun warms. Enveloped in pine trees we are again in the forest, the beautiful Thüringer Wald. Baby is lying in his carriage, and I am lying on soft thick moss sunning myself. The sky is dark blue, high and glorious. One must have visited hell to be able to see heaven as it really is.

The lovely spot is isolated from any path or road. I lifted the carriage and carried it through to it. How light the carriage has become.

Tall pines rustle. I take my shoes off and wade in clear water of a friendly stream. Sometimes I hear distant shooting or far-off whizzing of planes. My son has gotten rosy cheeks and looks so understanding, almost like a grown man.

Evening

Have just returned from the man with AKU radio. His wooden house is far up the hill in the forest near the cave where we hid at the first attacks.

Now I am somewhat oriented. Eastern and northern Berlin are under Russian artillery fire and are being bombed six times a night. Suburbs also. Perhaps here we suffer less than we would have if we had stayed? Yesterday, the Americans occupied Nuremberg. They are outside Dresden, Hamburg, Bremen. They approach Czechoslovakia. The Russian and American front will soon meet at many points.

21

Horrors in the Spreading Peace

Today I heard a new word—*Konzentrationslager* (Concentration Camp). One here, in Ohrdruf. Thousands of skeletons. Almost everyone starved to death or has been shot to death. It cries to the heavens. The terrified few still alive are all being set free, fed, clothed, healed. But nothing will ever heal their wounds, their terrible suffering—a suffering unknown to any who have not gone through it.

Leipzig and Halle are occupied. The Russians sit outside Dresden. All rails are destroyed. This war could be over in days.

Here, the rumbling and thundering continue. Columns of colossal trucks now laden with prisoners race through our woodland. But freed French prisoners of war drive through also. Green branches and garlands of flowers decorate these trucks on the way home to France. These vehicles drive, not race, and these "prisoners" sing, wave, and laugh.

April 24, 1945

I am so nauseated from that wet black bread, only and always black bread. No vegetables, butter, or bacon fat. Nothing. Our fat finds from the horse and sausages left behind were used up too soon. I begged the innkeeper's wife for some half-rotten carrots from the cellar.

And the Big War still isn't over and summons more victims every second. My husband could be in Berlin's terrible fighting and bombardment. A different kind of hell has broken loose there.

Ever more soldiers of the Reich, single ones and pairs, slowly shuffle through our valley. Usually clothed only in blue jeans or short torn pants, without a shirt, without papers, without weapons, without the least tool of war, they come tripping along in a line without end. Everybody shares with them what they can. Food or clothes. A coat here, a shirt there. Everybody shakes their hands, and heartfelt good wishes accompany them on the path to their destinies, their defeated walk home through the Great Reich.

Those who can still talk say the same things.

"Must first search for my wife, my children."

"If I can't find them anymore, life has no purpose."

"If I can't find them . . . it's all worthless."

"Now I must search."

This morning three stopped in front of the milk store on their way south to Munich. We shook hands, and our eyes were moist. They talked about the Americans and how friendly they were. "I even got a ride in their jeep," said one.

I gave another the address of my sister in Bavaria, and asked them to see her, to find her. Don't know if her street is still there, if she is still alive.

We watch them string through our village, and all of us wonder if husband—father—brother—son is one of them. Women now always look down the streets and more closely at many faces.

And I? Night and day, I think of him, where he could be, if he got our last message. I sent it through one of the men led by Frau Klein's lieutenant on his way to Berlin then. I wonder if he had the chance to walk away and find us. Maybe? Dear God, let it be.

April 26, 1945

It is cool and has rained incessantly. The tips of the hills are enshrouded in a white hue. Just when our roof had been fixed and covered, the rain started. Many free hands have been making a new sound nailing, sawing, repairing. Most roofs in our village are now mended.

Hunger is cruel. I must try Ohrdruf. But the roads are getting rougher because of the colossal trucks that take up the whole road. We duck into roadside ditches to not be pushed over. If only I had a bike.

April 27, 1945

Back from Ohrdruf, BY BIKE. Frau Klein asked friends to lend me a bike. I can have it again. Often the monster tanks and trucks almost clipped me, scary. But very successful, got bacon, one quarter pound. And a wonder: a pound of sugar, a pound of margarine, and a pound of cheese. Unbelievable. All for ration stamps.

April 28, 1945

Last night in bed at nine and slept through until six. My son began to talk and kick at six. He kicked everything about, even his play-suit, and romped and threw himself about loudly and happily.

Life is beautiful.

Afternoon

We are quite high up on the Kienberg in the forest and settled close to the mountain road. Down there is Schwartzbach, a toy-town with little toy-houses and church. Peace is all pervading. I took my notebook to write about yesterday evening.

I went to the man with the AKU radio and listened with many others. The Russians have half of Berlin. Street fighting on Unter den Linden. It is a main street, a once pompous street, the city's showpiece, the military parade ground from the Kaisers to Hitler. Only notables lived on that street in its sumptuous buildings. The people of Berlin have no water. I think of the babies and mothers. Goebbels—I hate writing his name—demands that women and children fight. Whoever refuses will be shot. Anyone who dares to raise the white flag will be shot. They said Hitler himself is fighting.

Two returned soldiers sit a little farther up. I bring them some bread that I now always carry with me. Down in the valley, the river Ohra glistens like silver. The meadows look newly painted, and little puppets with diligent hands are busy on the roofs of houses wiping away the traces of war.

The fresh green hills and so many blossoms open my heart, prepare me to be happy again. But all the people around us are so downhearted. Deep inside I am as happy as I have been in a long time, despite the worry for our Papa. With every Allied victory I become happier. Perhaps a time to live freely will come soon.

Oh, dear little boy, we laugh so much together, laugh for relief and hope. We love all things good and beautiful. Look around you, my son. The world is immense—and God *is*. Look up and around, and down there—let it rumble.

Yes, down there it rolls and rumbles again. Tanks upon tanks, armored cars, trucks, artillery. Column after column, a giant steel stream.

On the way back, we met the nurse who visited Georg in his illness. "He came out of it very well." She told me about mines in the woods, that we shouldn't, under any circumstances, go too far into the forest. Well, we have had a guardian angel once more, had been far in several times, so peaceful there.

Salzburg and its Reichenhall have been bombed. That's where I went to school. Salzburg and bombs—I can't imagine it.

April 29, 1945

Outside it is storming and snowing. The sky boils your diapers. I no longer have any laundry soap.

Shall I write it down? Is it legitimate premonition or only desire? I feel that he, your father and my husband, will come soon, very soon. Mad wishing or a premonition, I have no way to know.

While Georg sunbathed, he turned over all by himself. What wonderful progress, and lying on his stomach is a special joy. Every day he is becoming handsomer. In the morning I often take him over into my bed. Sometimes we both fall asleep.

He is wearing his first nightie. A kindly seamstress made it for money. They don't accept money in the city anymore. It's all worthless, they say. In the city, it would have cost at least a quarter pound of bacon, and that's about one hundred marks today. Also, today there was butter for babies, a quarter pound. Yesterday evening for the first time in a long time I sang a little song, the French melody, "Vous et Moi," and Georg fell asleep.

Money

Here at our Good Fairy's we are still paying rent with the worthless money, fifteen marks a month. It's very little and almost the same as in peacetime. A good spirit must have whispered to go to the bank in Berlin, which was still standing then, and made me withdraw a large sum. We will survive a bit longer with it—but what then? After this big war, there won't be any banks, and my bundle of marks gets smaller and more worthless day by day.

But my son is with me, and that gives me courage and strength. His first steps? The little shoes are waiting. The mayor's daughter stopped me on the street and told me they have found a large shoe depot near here, that she had reserved white leather baby shoes for me. She asked if I want them. And how I want them, a wonderful surprise to get those tiny, little shoes. How and who made them I have no idea but am amazed at these little tokens of peace, normalcy.

The mayor's daughter continued. "You never belonged to *them*? Am I right? My father could see it, that you were lying, that you were never the wife of an OT commander. You can't imagine how difficult this time was for my father, how happy and relieved he is now. Many opposed the Nazis. But as mayor it was awfully hard. One never knows who will turn us in."

It is afternoon, and my son is asleep. I am sitting in the kitchen alone. Frau Klein is with her relatives. It's storming outside. The forest shines through the windows and roars as the ocean. The tall pines bend in the windstorm. There are many, many stumps among them, as with men. Many white splotches in the green ocean.

April 30, 1945

On the radio: In Berlin hell is still loose. The madness continues.

Hand-to-hand combat. Now children are fighting too, in Charlottenburg and Dahlem. Mussolini has been captured at the Swiss border. Milan and Bremen occupied. Goering has fled, said the radio. It must end soon.

Got some sauerkraut from the innkeeper's wife, enough for one meal. A human being needs so much to eat. I am always cold and weak. I still have some flour—brought with us from Berlin. Every morning I mix a bit of it with water and stir it into a pan and fry it brown without any oil or fat or butter. There is none.

And yet, I am grateful for every hour without fear of bombs and shells.

I would like so very much to talk to someone about gains and losses in spirit after such experiences, about nostalgia, love, courage, egotism.

But I must hurry, cook porridge, get the diapers up from the backyard as wet and cold as they are.

May 1, 1945

One degree below freezing. Now in May! The ring of iron around my heart tightens. Many thoughts, no sleep.

The town's butcher hanged himself. They stole his cattle right from under his nose. It was in Ohrdruf. His truck stood in front of a store. He saw the men and tried to save his precious livestock. They beat him up and knocked him out. He was sixty-five.

I met the brewery coachman. He once gave me a ride to Ohrdruf. He said, "When I saw our soldiers, and then the Americans, I knew we were being lied to. I saw it with my own eyes. A Negro gave my little one, she is five years old, a can of cocoa. I didn't know of anything that good even before the war."

Noon, at the man with the AKU. Many were there to listen. The latest: the Americans are fighting in Allgäu. Mussolini was shot and hung upside down in the city of Milan as a public showcase. A sign attached to his body read: "This is a just punishment." Hitler may be dead. Goebbels shot himself, his wife and six children. Munich surrendered without further fighting. In Italy, the Americans are marching towards the Brenner. They are about to occupy Hamburg and have Mecklenburg. The last corners and borders of the Great Reich stand before the *Endsieg* (Hitler's hourly watchword). Himmler has announced the capitulation of Germany to England and America. This miserable scoundrel. That delay by these criminals, they know well there is no legitimate capitulation without including Russia. In the meantime, every hour hundreds of men, women, and children are slaughtered.

The Russians in combat on the Kurfürstendamm, and Halensee where I have lived and worked. Ninety percent of Berlin conquered—all concentration camps opened, more atrocities discovered—horror upon horror.

My son, as soon as we can, we shall leave this part of the globe. I have always felt better outside of this country that manufactured all the madness.

May 3, 1945

There was an official radio announcement that Hitler fell in combat, that Dönitz, his successor, will continue to fight. The propaganda gives that monster, as a fallen soldier, a heroic departure.

The Americans now have all the south: Mittenwald, Garmisch, Oberammergau, Passau, not much left.

In the afternoon, the parish priest suddenly appeared in the kitchen door to see Frau Klein. He sat and talked and talked. "To talk finally free," as he put it, and that he can at last say what he had always thought about our regime, about these murderers.

Dear old Frau Klein visibly shrank. Her world collapsed. During the last days she must have often heard the Nazis condemned but deep inside couldn't believe it, what others said about them. Now, the priest himself concurred. It surely must be true. Her cheeks, usually red, turned white.

It is so cold that Georg holds onto his blanket and has stopped kicking about. No heat in the house. He is a half year old today. No toy.

22

May 6, 1945

Georg begins to grasp things. Trembling all over, he stretches and strains as though he would turn over a mighty rock. Or he cautiously reaches out for my red scarf which I hung over his Betti. When it then falls onto his face, he yells in amusement and delight.

It's Sunday again and we are alone. While I did the dishes and washed diapers, I sang my little boy to sleep. He loves when I sing to him.

Got two boxes of rotten carrots that I sorted and cleaned. Now they lie out in the garden and are getting washed by our endless rain.

Two days ago, a man came into the kitchen to visit Frau Klein. She introduced him as "Herr Berg." He came, he said, to invite me to his home for coffee. He explained he had been the supervisor of the cave. I didn't recognize him.

He said, "I must apologize that I took you into my arms that morning, but I felt so sorry for you. You could no longer speak. You were unable to utter sound."

I had no memory of this embrace or of my lost voice.

I visited the Bergs yesterday. His wife was there and a man who looked like a ghost, who had just been freed from a concentration camp.

The man spoke of hunger worse than what we have experienced, one pound of bread for five days. Of thirst, five days without water. Thousands burned alive. "I can't talk about it . . . I can't talk about many things . . . never," he said.

The more we are afflicted the tighter become our lips. May our Lord bless him. We compare our land with others and are deeply depressed. Not until recent days had I heard of such horrors.

They find dead soldiers deep in the forest, a few every day. The town's funeral bell whines twice a day—for soldiers, suicides, fatal accidents.

Oh, for the time when people shall again die a natural death? I pray that my son grows into a better world. I pray that I may lead him out of this into a free land. *Ein Land das Gott anschaut.* A land that God looks at.

May 7, 1945

Perhaps it's silly to write about it, but now that everything in over, I yearn for beautiful things, for the best comforts in this uncomfortable world. For a bath, for happy faces. When Georg shouts for joy, it's a message to have patience and more patience. If only I had something to eat or wine to warm.

Longing for vivacity. Almost every night for six years now, I've huddled in these miserable cellars shaking with fear. I am done with being afraid. Why must we sit among hills in a tiny chamber, hungry, cold, not knowing where to go, what to do? I would like to dress up, beautifully. No more scrubbing and washing and fleeing and begging for food. Oh, to not be hungry. For that all to be over, and yet the chains around me, around us, remain unbroken. I would like to be in Paris and buy hats.

But I must be sensible. Paris is no longer as it was then ... We must find your Dad, or he must find us. We can't stay here much longer.

If only the sun would come out again, the great consoler. Nature, the only, the great comforter.

Herr Berg gave me some books, one about Cairo, where I had been to make that movie. How long ago was it? A hundred years?

May 8, 1945

News. In Denmark, Norway, Holland, armistices. Bells ring, people dance in the streets. The same in Italy. Only in Czechoslovakia fighting goes on with the SS.

May 9, 1945

Two at night complete capitulation of Germany! At last! At last! The final fighting took place in Prague's suburbs.

In England, bells chime, they pray, dance, and celebrate. The same in America, but not so much in Moscow—too war-weary and shocked. And with the end, the sun came out and warmth.

May 11, 1945

It is seven in the evening. You are lying in your Betti, relaxed and tanned and so tired from the pure forest air, from all your sightseeing, fast asleep and contented.

So many new green leaves rustled in the wind. A little stream glistened and gurgled through the meadow on which you lay. A little girl kept you company. She is three years old and was so busy putting tiny green twigs into your fingers. Her mother, Linda, the strange woman who shared her bed with us after the cave, was there too.

She walked through the forest with her new friend, an "Ami" (American soldier). He looks nice, and things are getting back to normal.

May 12, 1945

Now, that we have peace, sunshine, the forest and tranquility, where is he? I am on the lookout all the time. Thinking, now he must come. By foot. On a bike from this way or that. Right at this moment somebody might be asking the innkeeper. Always listening for his voice.

I discover myself putting on make-up and sort of dressing up, as far as I can do that here. Every morning my first thought is TODAY! Or I stand at the bend in the road and look out and look out until my eyes hurt. A few times I forgot my chores and hurried back home.

My listening and watching must be a symptom of madness. He can't know where we are. We said we would meet in my sister's place in Bayern. He would never know to stop here, to look for us among the few local families who survived the battle of Stutzhaus, who stayed here.

If only I could talk with someone about these things but can't find anyone to talk to. Today, I met the local parson in the milk shop. Maybe I can talk to him, I thought. His face was yellow and dry as straw. His sermons are ingenious and arresting.

He talked of the last days. "Three generals took up quarters in my parish house. Now it's like a sieve from the shells. The first general, Herr von G., said: 'What is now left for me? My son has fallen, my house in ashes, my sister, who married a Jew, starved to death in a concentration camp. The second general locked himself into my cellar with a few men. They roistered through the nights. I couldn't find shelter in my own cellar. So, I ran to the cave-shelter at night.

"The next day the Herr General was gone, the wine was gone too, and the box with the offerings. The third general ordered the bridges demolished and thought he could stop the war here in Stutzhaus, stop the war with America.

"I am through, done."

I left the store after him, still pondering. A woman approached him and told him about her rabbits, that they don't eat properly. No, I couldn't talk to the priest, too much to say.

May 14, 1945

When in the forest, we always collect pine cones. We don't go in far anymore. These cones warm the kitchen stove quickly and well. Our loyal war comrade, the brave carriage, climbs every rough mountain road, toils over gnarled ground squeaking happily in all its joints.

We got four ounces of butter and a big bunch of sprouted spinach for stamps.

I read there are three million Americans in Germany, four hundred thousand will stay in occupation.

Many robberies in town and in the vicinity. Big and little ones. They have broken into our house twice since we've moved back. But each time they got caught. "They are after the innkeeper's pig," said Frau Klein.

May 16, 1945

I had to go with Georg to Ohrdruf. It was hot today, suddenly hot now. The doctor wanted to see him, and I tried to get some food. I asked about transportation for us out of here and to Bavaria or . . . ? All the way along, I thought we would meet our Papa, convinced that we'd meet him suddenly on the road.

At the town hall, a Pole, a Frenchman, and a German girl happily chatted as if there had never been a war. A picture of European togetherness. The Frenchman still wore his striped prison uniform.

Huge placards at the town hall's entrance. Photos of heaps of corpses from Ohrdruf's concentration camp with the caption: ALL OF YOU should know!

May 18, 1945

It is hard to write down how everything hurts, every fiber, a sensation of shrinking. And always this iron ring around my heart and ache from hunger. No nourishment, no wine, no cigarette, no fruit, nothing. No radio, and no light yet. The best is the forest, and we go there almost every day.

The fields lie bare and empty. No one will sow. No seeds. No one home to sow.

On the roads, men keep coming and going. They come walking eight hundred kilometers from Italy, over the Alps, over snow and ice, five hundred kilometers from Hungary, from Berlin two hundred fifty kilometers away, from the Rhine, from Munich three hundred kilometers. Skeletons in rags. They shuffle over mountains, through the woods. For this they talked of BLOOD and HONOR over twelve years. The survivors now sneak through the land, wretched, hurt, and hungry. Men have become vagrants, women lamenters.

One of these men came into Frau Klein's kitchen. A colonel. He had once stayed in her apartment during the war. He too had walked four hundred kilometers from the north, heading for Magdeburg, his home. He looked like all of them and fell over some potatoes, devoured them like a starving wolf. The colonel for whom no one will ever again stand at attention.

Austria and Czechoslovakia freed yesterday.

New monstrous war-transport-trucks still drive through town, this time loaded with Russians. All of them wave red flags. The women wear bright red scarves, and flowers adorn the truck sides. They are being driven home, and they too sing.

You are now able to sit upright and turn around, right, left, sure and alive and high-spirited. You can hold up your little head quite well. Before, it always tilted like a withered flower. For five weeks your ears had suppurated, and your Mommy Doctor cleaned them twice a day with cotton and peroxide. Every other day calcium in your food, and every day rubbing big carrots and squeezing carrots and searching and begging for new carrots so that you would never be deprived of this curative juice. Every day Vigantol drops except during the worst war days. The doctor in Ohrdruf gave us his highest praise.

Do you know that you are quite a special boy? Other babies fall asleep with their thumbs in their mouth or with a rubber teat. Not you. You prefer a diaper of the finest quality, rejecting rougher material. Hugging it close like a doll one tip in your mouth, you go to sleep.

23

One More Kind Stranger

May 27, 1945

A hard rain falls and makes our valley fume and steam and chokes the heart.

I can hardly hold myself upright. We receive two ounces of bacon fat a week. Nothing else. Our carrots are all gone too. I must go hoarding. Among Father's things here is a pair of new shoes. Perhaps I can barter them, though rather poor small landholders make up the communities of Stutzhaus and Schwarzbach. With a small plot of land or a small woodlot, five cows at the most and a few chickens. But I'll try.

A farmer might give us some foodstuff for shoes he does not need. Farmers are collecting all kinds of useful things. That is called *hamstern* (hoarding), my son.

Lately, I have not recorded much, and not for many days. The days all seem the same, or am I too hungry, too tired, worn down to notice anything change? Concentrating, making my hands move a pencil on paper has become so hard. Do I look like those men stumbling through the land in search of a past, reaching for imagined loved ones who might be only ghosts?

Lately, I have been talking to myself like a schoolgirl talks to herself about tasks that a teacher or parent gave her, simple tasks that must get done. "Breathe the forest air deeply. It is clean. Sleep. It is deep. Look at your son. He is alive. And believe that we'll be transplanted one of these days. Until then bear it, do the thing that must be done next," I talk and think over and over.

I still seek out the latest news at the man with the AKU. The English and Americans talk about our famine, talk about Germany as a sick, evil child. They are right, gruesomely so.

Late Evening

Linda, the strange woman, came by this evening. I hardly recognized her, so radiantly beautiful had she become.

She talked about her lot. Her husband has fallen. Her home in Cologne has been destroyed. She found refuge here in Stutzhaus at her grandmother's. Her little daughter, the one who played with Georg, came with her. Mama, who is twenty-five, is the perfect likeness of her daughter. She put a few oranges and tomatoes on the kitchen table, and a few of those glistening army cans with butter and cheese.

I cried and cried. I cry too easily.

"I too want to go to Berlin," she says. "Maybe we should trek to Berlin together. My aunt lives there, and my man is getting transferred to near there."

If her aunt's home is still inhabitable, Linda will take us in until we have found Papa, or he has found us. Her eyes shine. Love? Luck? She doesn't talk about it. I wish her happiness with all my heart.

Hope.

Linda carries her burdens well, better than I carry mine. Banden (gangs) chased Linda's grandfather into the woods and ripped off his clothes. He came home naked. Banden took a carriage from a woman Linda knows and dumped the child onto the street.

Linda leaves hastily. It is almost dark. Yes, the curfew was moved from seven to nine.

I look out the window after her. It is still light, and the sky is high. Swallows soar up higher and higher, up into the light blue sky.

May 28, 1945

We are in the inn's gazebo out in the garden. It is old and damaged, but it still stands there with all its worn romance. Baby is lying in his carriage, and I am sitting on the bench, of which not much is left. Out on the *Hauptstrasse* (Main Street) now and again a truck races through the village.

People are on their Sunday stroll, dressed in their church clothes walking along calmly. Linda comes by, next to her the Ami. He too wears a dark suit with bright tie. If he were not so healthy and cheerful and polite, he could be German. He smiles at Linda often and she at him.

A wren approaches our gazebo, flying through the broken window, with a fat insect in its beak for the baby wren. There! It looks out of the nest, an old embroidered satchel hanging on the wall.

And my little one? He is working hard, lying on his back wanting to raise his head, clenching his fists and using all his strength. I take him onto my lap, and he looks around and around so terribly cleverly and curiously.

Our wren approaches several times before it dares to fly in. To find our nest again. Dear Lord, that is all I ask now.

Part IV

The Trek

From a July 1938 magazine feature article on
"The Actress Katharina Berger"

24

Milk and Bullets

Waiting is no longer bearable. Babies only get one quarter litre of milk now. Same with vegetables. All food the authorities collect first goes to camp survivors. Trains don't yet run. That's all I could learn when I inquired about leaving.

I'll have to go to Gotha, the nearest and largest city in this county. There we might find a trace. There we might find Papa. His last duty posts were all on the Russian front east of Berlin.

He might be waiting for us in the house in Kladow. He might have fled to my sister in Bavaria. But I can't strike out for Bavaria on my own. I must take Linda's help. Daddy might be lying ill or injured wanting to see his son, needing me. Maybe there is not much time. Maybe . . . maybe . . . Berlin is the only place for me to find work again. And it's not that far, really. Need to start somewhere, somehow.

That is why we must head into the street again.

Good night, my darling. May our Lord keep you and guard you.

May 29, 1945

The sun is out again in its full glory—the great consoler.

161

Long ride with baby, a hoarding ride, to a farmer who lives deep in the forest where the valley narrows to a footpath, where the dense firs become a dome, high, dark and scented. As always in this forest, the pine perfume pervades, but here, in this dome, it is overwhelming.

It is late, 9:30 p.m.

There was nothing at that farmer. He only wanted to give milk for new shoes. As usual, I collected fir cones to fill up the carriage. So good to heat bathwater. And the light is on. The radio works too. Herr Berg was here and left another book for me. I have not looked at it, too tired, too hungry.

June 1, 1945

A few houses had to be vacated. A few Americans moved in.

We got coffee! Real coffee! One hundred grams. And tea, ten grams.

We two were on the road this afternoon and ran into a thunderstorm. Just then as we drove through a field, detonations. Horribly close, again and again. I pulled the carriage into the nearest ditch, filled with water and mud. Couldn't get it out again.

After a time, a man came by. I had to ask him for help. He pointed to the forest, they blew up the subterranean munition depots, he said. Precisely where we had wanted to go this afternoon.

In the evening, when Georg was asleep, I borrowed the bike and tried another farmer. He liked the shoes and gave me milk, one pound of bacon, and three eggs! How long has it been? He must have taken pity on me—or was enthralled by you. Every other day, I may come for milk, he said. His milk is so creamy I can skim off the top and fry with it. So glad.

June 2, 1945

And where is my husband? At times the ring around my heart expands as though it would breathe. Most times it presses tighter from day to day. Found a bundle of his old letters. Can't read them. In the new book from Herr Berg there is a passage where parents are together with their child. I couldn't read on.

I am not very brave.

Baby is asleep under the apple tree next to the gazebo. The sun twinkles through white mountains of cumulus. The wren again feeds its young. It now curiously stretches its head out of the satchel.

How will we two get to Berlin? How get to a home? Will there be a theatre again? Do my so painstakingly nailed boxes still exist? Will there be a message from Papa in one of them as we had planned? By winter we must find each other.

Every day someone makes his way back home to our area. Yesterday a teacher from Schwarzbach, then one more local man and another.

Since the shoe barter for milk, I feel a bit better. We can get beer, with three percent alcohol. The Americans ordered the brewery reopened. The inn's beer room is back to peacetime operation with smoke, men, and loud political exchanges. The brewery was always the King of Stutzhaus. It had been owned by Frau Klein's late husband, and now by his brother, the "relatives."

I am now especially privileged, because each night our Fairy presents me with a glass of good beer, brewed for the Americans only with an even higher percentage of alcohol!

June 3, 1945

My son is seven months old today. The sun embraces the cool forest in Sunday glitter. Our valley is quiet and empty; everyone is in church. We two are on our way into the forest.

Later

This morning in the woods not far from the main street, I saw two men rummaging through a huge scrap heap, stirring through hundreds of shiny cans and boxes. When they saw us, they looked up half smiling and half guilty, their arms loaded with fatty meat. They washed it at a nearby spring. I approached and looked at that scrap heap.

White bread in paper bags, loaves and loaves. They took it all, but handed me three loaves, such a gift. I have never seen such fine white bread, waste from another continent.

I will soak it in milk for my son. It will make many wonderful meals.

Little reliefs. The loaves of bread. A strange exotic flower on the windowsill. The sun and the trees.

When I awake in the morning, two tanned little legs kick about between the railings of his Betti, a happy grin on his face. Besides, his Betti is complete again with fine new bars. A cabinetmaker from next door fixed it.

June 9, 1945

One month after the capitulation.

I came home late from my walk to the farmer in the forest for milk. One hour walk there and one hour back. I couldn't get the bike today, almost didn't get back at all. Oh, my dearest son. What a world has grown around you.

When I returned to the main street with the milk, it was late but still light. I remembered blackberry bushes now covered by sweet ripe berries quite close to the street, and turned into the woods for them, bent down into the bushes when—tschee—tschee—tschee. Three shots dead-sharp at me!

I ran and ran, crashed through the bushes, staggered through branches and over roots, wandered around. How long I don't know.

Suddenly he stood in front of me. The sniper. I looked into a cold, ugly face, a thin strip for a mouth, a nose long and sharp, eyes like buttons, dirty clothes hanging on a skeleton frame. He stretched his hand out towards me, full of bullets.

"Good for you," he said with an accent I could not place, from some other country or region in the east. He might have been Russian.

I flew away, home.

Is it war madness? A lunatic? Is it whisky? Is it . . . ? I don't know. I only know that I did get home, perhaps seconds before the curfew. My skirt has two bullet holes in it.

June 22, 1945

I have been ill. Fever for two days, but I'm not surprised. A body, my body, has limits. That shooter took me past mine.

Linda has been very good to me. We will join up when she is ready to go to Berlin. "As soon as there is the slightest opportunity for some kind of transportation," she said. "Maybe he only wanted to scare you," she said before she left.

And my son grows wonderfully, tanned cheeks, tanned little knees. His galli-galli stories become louder and funnier. And I bought a crate of carrots. A kind neighbor brought Vigantol, his most important medicine from Ehrfurt (a large city). She went there by truck.

Our town crier brought news too. "The blackout is lifted, the blackout is lifted."

June 24, 1945

The summer world smells of hay, and we got a gift. Strawberries! Frau Klein brought them to Georg from her little garden. "The very first ones," she said.

Women in gay scarves balance hay in huge baskets on their heads. And I bathed in some cool, deep trout brook. Yes, summer is here.

In a few days a truck will go to Gotha. I secured a spot on it. I must inquire how we can best get to Berlin.

25

Finding a Way to Leave

June 25, 1945

War's aftermath: A farmer with wagon and horse blew high into the air in the woods. Whole areas are sown with mines, and no one knows where.

Radio news: Ribbentrop, the bomb-sure one, has finally been caught in a pension in Hamburg carrying a knapsack full of money. Another Nazi big shot, Robert Ley, caught in a cellar in Berchtesgaden. They'll all go to hell and can no longer find a hideout anywhere.

Our house got a returned soldier. The innkeeper's son! "Now only two are missing. My daughter's husband and my brother," he says.

June 26, 1945

The truck for Gotha will leave at the end of the week.

I can hardly write, too hard. I'm too weak and can't concentrate. Must keep up. We must get through to Berlin, or to my sister. We need a home and work. My son needs care. His precious supply of

167

food cans is shrinking. Our money bundle is worth less every day. Farmers get offers of five hundred marks for a pound of butter.

Went on an outing with Georg, Linda, and her daughter. I told her about my work, my beloved theatre. So good to talk about these things.

She told me about her Ami, Tom. "He speaks a little German. His grandparents came from here." After a while she continues, "Tom is really very nice and so good to Barbara (her little daughter), but I can't believe everything he tells me. When he talks about America and how good they live there. It's just too much, can't be true."

I believe what Tom tells her. Too many who have lived there, worked there, tell of the same life in America, of its cities, and farms and food, and the generosity of its people.

We walked on. "But then, he is quite serious. He's from a farm in Ohio. He showed me a picture. Very big, big house and barn."

June 27, 1945

We went to Ohrdruf. I got a perm and saw myself in the mirror, closely, and was shocked. I do look like some of the wandering men. But my little one does not notice, smiles at me often.

The diapers hang outside night and day. The wind and rain and sun are the only laundry soap.

June 29, 1945

I am writing this in Gotha, in a restaurant, in a city without fear of alarms.

Fields of ruins, soldiers, war vehicles of all sizes, tanks, jeeps zoom by on dusty streets. Rubble, throngs of people. An American sentry at the railroad station tells me of the first train today to the city of Ehrfurt. So, we can make it to Ehrfurt for sure.

Went to the garrison's headquarters and saw the commandant. "I would like to ask for some spot for me and my baby on any transport to Berlin," I said and tried to explain in English, as well as I could, the urgency of our departure.

"Are you not afraid?"

I laughed, "Why?"

"*So müsten alle Deutschen sein,*" he answered in German. "*Dann wäre vieles leichter.*" (All Germans should be that way. Then many things would be easier.)

He explained he couldn't give me a permit through the Russian Zone, which we would have to cross on our trek to Berlin. The American Zone has been sealed off about 100 kilometers from here at the Russian territory. But farther on it becomes American territory again. To get to Berlin we surely will have to go through the Russian Zone. As things stand, we can't risk it.

And my son? Will he be all right, all day without Mommy, but with all his pans and spoons and food cans? Today he is staying with Linda.

I must write more about my ways in a city. Also went to the local German government. There I talked to a *Regierungsrat* (administrative adviser). "Camp" was written all over him. Clipped hair, his clothes hanging on a shrunken body, trembling hands. Tiredly, he suggested I talk to the Americans.

Before our truck with trailer, its boxes, vegetables, and human bundles returned into the rain, I went "shopping." A piece of cord for our broken trunk, genuine cord, a few pounds of vegetables for ration stamps, and a little margarine. I got a thermometer for baby's bathwater.

In a little antique shop, squeezed among ruins, I found a beautiful picture, an old print. Jesus, by Leonardo Da Vinci. He looks young, kind, and caring. I already heard myself saying to my son, "See, that is Jesus." The art dealer will get it framed, and I will pick it up next time.

I made it back by seven in the evening.

June 30, 1945

I wash my Georg, wash his coat, then all his sheets. Once, twice, and again and again. My dearest has been throwing up since yesterday evening. Today three times. Oh, if I only hadn't left him alone in my searches for food and information.

July 2, 1945

The Russians are coming.

The Americans are withdrawing with a big racket, as if with one big boom. Giant trucks once again rumble through the valley without interruption. These monsters almost threw me over on my way for the milk, this time on a bike.

Yesterday, many evacuated persons from Düsseldorf on the Rhine, who sheltered here in Stutzhaus during the war, headed back to what they hope will still be standing and to relatives they might find.

Transport permits out of here have been distributed by alphabet and age. Many will be left behind to wait for more permits or whatever else comes here. There is great lamenting, because the locals all fear Russians will soon shut off the border. This new Russian Zone will spread far into the county of Thüringen, far beyond Eisenach. Those left behind don't know when the next transport will go and where. Not many trucks left for civilians after this war. Nor do they know if they ever will get across the new border once the Russians clamp hold.

But we have a transport permit, and for us the road is open now, also for our Papa if he can find someone to give him a permit, if he is in condition to ask for it, he'll get a permit too. He'll make his way to a safe part of Berlin, I know it. He must.

We can't wait too long. All is too uncertain with these Zones and new borders and with the Russians.

July 5, 1945

My dearest darling, you are ill. After every meal you throw up—and now diarrhea too. When I hold you up to sit, you collapse. Went to the nurse. "An epidemic broke out among babies and young children."

You can only have oatmeal and saccharine. Now you must starve too.

The Aftermath of War

A strange truck stopped at the mayor's house and loaded up with all there was, furniture, clothes, dishes—everything down to the last spoon. And this in the middle of the day. It is the third house emptying in Stutzhaus since the war's end. All weapons had to be surrendered, first to the Nazi soldiers, then to the Americans. The bandits have machine guns.

The mayor's daughter now has one nightgown, nothing else. I brought her a dress and some underwear. Pale as a ghost, she told me she had to raise her hands and watch the bandits pack up.

An anti-bandit method has been developed. It begins with the crier. He goes through the village with his bell and shouts out as soon as the bad deeds have begun. Then the siren is supposed to sound. I wonder if the siren can sound soon enough. They say someone will be on watch, and as soon as he hears the crier or screaming, he'll push the alarm button.

But what if he doesn't hear the screaming? Because the bandits are busy looting in Schwarzbach behind the hills, and the siren is at the train station in Stutzhaus? Or what if the watchman does hear the screaming, the siren sounds, and all the brave men meet at the bridge (that's the plan) armed with sticks, shovels and axes, then run to that spot from whence the screams were heard to find the crime already complete? I couldn't help but laugh at all that.

July 6, 1945

The Russians have arrived. They've already shot seventy-five bandits in the vicinity, it is said. I hope they were bandits and not desperate men on their way home. That might explain why house emptying and wagon thefts seem to have waned.

Two very young chaps in dirty Russian uniforms play with a bicycle. Get up. Get down, ride in circles. Get up again. Then both get on it, visibly delighted about the bicycle marvel.

Three impressions I will never forget

The German soldiers.
Shattered. An almighty mass of wretchedness seeping out of every-where, out of the forest, the ground, buildings and huts, like a foul underground river coming out. It sweeps everything along—the lost glory, the blood, the Honor and Bravery, the Iron Crosses and now wooden crosses on makeshift graves, too many to count. Crosses

over bodies after no funeral, no notice to family or friends. By the time anyone found living relatives, the piled-up corpses would rot.

The American soldiers.
Like a football team on the way to the match. Young, calm, unburdened. Equipped to the teeth, but always helpful, friendly.

The Russian soldiers.
They came quietly. I only heard of a GPU (Russian Secret Police) in Ohrdruf, of the seventy-five bandit executions. Then the young bicycle amateurs. The next day, three Russian officers highly decorated with glittering medals entered our town. Then nothing for days. Quiet. Then here a car with a lone soldier, there a car with soldiers, mysterious.

July 10, 1945

No milk for my ration card today. The driver is dead, beaten to death. His truck with the milk and butter has vanished.

Last night the robber-siren! I watched from the window. It took a while for the men to assemble, each holding a stick or shovel. Nothing more happened, nothing to do with the milk truck driver. Someone must have screamed at a mouse. And no Russian soldier in our village went after these new bandits.

July 21, 1945

In Gotha with my son, to see a children's doctor. We came by train, which has been running for a few days now. The railroad officer in a clean blue uniform looked happy—back to normal again.

The doctor's waiting room crammed. After hours he saw us.

The verdict: Georg must not eat, just water and saccharin. At least I'll give him some carrot juice. Otherwise he'll starve to death. He is so weak already. On a bench in front of Gotha's famous castle, now demolished, I changed his diaper.

Colorful Russian banners, placards, and signs glare down from Gotha's ruins, streetcorners, roofs, somewhat brightening up the dusty rubble heap of a city. Larger than life-sized pictures of Stalin, excerpts from his speeches about War and Life in giant letters.

I inquire about getting to Berlin. It is true. One can get to Berlin, if one can find transportation. In a restaurant I hear a woman whisper in an urgent voice offering her wedding ring to be taken along. Yes, we could go by train to Berlin but only stage by stage. It will take about two weeks for the 250 kilometers, so close and yet so far away.

The little cardboard carriage with baby accompanies me on my road.

At the last, after doing everything I had to do, we went back to the antique shop, to the once-famous art dealer of Berlin. A little chat. He remembered seeing me in a play. Our Jesus is beautifully framed, and I showed Him to Georg. But his little eyes would not focus, so tired, so dim with fever and hunger.

I got more precious information. "Yes, you can go by train to Bitterfeld," said the art dealer. "But you'll have to change trains maybe a dozen times; then in Bitterfeld, you'll have to walk about fifteen kilometers to the Elbe. All bridges are blown up. Rowboats will take you across. About three hundred persons are brought across in one day. It's outrageously expensive. Maybe thousands are waiting to be taken over. And as it is now, there will soon be thousands more because Berlin has been shut off. An epidemic broke out."

We will wait. Patiently. We will accept our little forest recluse. And do everything to get my son well.

26

Trains

July 17, 1945

Georg, my dearest bundle, we are on the road to Berlin.

Linda wanted to leave. We know that I couldn't make that trek alone with baby and baggage, not more than a day, perhaps a day and the night. Then I would have to start dropping things we needed, like the ones who fled from the east with your uncle. It was a terribly hard decision because my baby is not yet well, but she could not wait.

The Gotha railroad station platform glows in the summer sun. All is enveloped by dust, dirt. Dusty grey bundles of humans with bags, sacks, crates push and scuffle. Our urgent necessities are too much on this road. I left our trunk filled with many things behind.

When a train will run no one knows. Whether we'll get a place on that train we don't know.

Georg is naked, almost, just covered by a soft diaper, lying in his cardboard box—our brave companion. And, as he has so often in difficult times, he shows a darling, consoling disposition.

Just hope the carriage wheels will hold. Many broken spokes rattle.

Once upon a time there was a forest, a spring and a wren. We could not stay there with the Russians closing in and the Americans gone. Home. Home? Where will it be?

July 18, 1945

In Ehrfurt.

We arrived in the evening, dirty, sweaty and dead tired. From Gotha to here is about thirty kilometers, and it took a whole day. We had to wait many hours for that train. Then again, it took many hours to get there standing in the stock car.

Here at the train station someone advised us to go to the hospital for quarters. Late in the evening, we rolled the carriage through this strange, ruined city. I pushed the carriage with one hand and with the other carried a large suitcase. Linda lugged a suitcase in one hand and in the other many bags. We came upon a big ruin, the former hospital.

Somewhere in that dark skeleton we encountered a nurse in uniform, a fat woman with a crude suspicious manner. I wanted to say, "Please give us a nook for the night. My baby is ill. Maybe we can get a place without draft where there is a cardboard window." I couldn't get out a word. All my firmness melted to tears.

Linda took over and negotiated.

We got the corner with the cardboard window. We got straw and blankets, we got warm water for the child, a thing of great value. I washed Georg, made him as comfortable as I could without anything to eat.

Then, I went back out onto the road and searched, for whole houses still standing, for people from whom I could borrow a strainer and grater for carrot juice. I begged from house to house.

In the third one, after a detailed explanation, I got a grater. I gave my wristwatch as security. Insignificant kitchen utensils are irrecoverable and expensive. With boundless need everywhere, everybody keeps what he can find, what he can get.

July 19, 1945

All day again rolling along in the stock-car. At dark, our train came to a final stop. A voice said, *"Das ist Sangershuasen."* My watch (I got it back when I returned the grater) showed 12:01 a.m.

Dazed, we found ourselves in the middle of nowhere. Sangershausen seems to be a tiny village. The dark hulks of solitary farmhouses sit along the edges of fields. We couldn't wander and beg now. No door would open for us. Farm dogs would challenge us. We sat down on the floor in the train station, a wooden platform under four posts supporting a wooden roof in the dark, in the open.

After a while, Linda or I or maybe both of us spotted a light not far away down the tracks. We didn't know what it was, but we marched to it.

An old man opened to our knock and let us in. Because of the baby, he said. It's the signalman's shack. We can stretch out on the floor. I can wash Georg and we even get some potatoes, which the man boils for us on a tiny iron stove. First meal in days. The man assures us that the train will leave at five in the morning, and we'd better be on it.

In the stock-car again with the heavy iron sliding doors open on both sides. A terribly bad draft for Georg. He is feverish and quite ill. I changed him four times in one hour. I am troubled.

179

We wait and wait, and the train doesn't move. We finally leave Sangershausen at nine. In one hand I hold onto one of those iron rings to which cattle are chained, with the other hand I hold onto the carriage. Linda sits on our luggage. We alternate. At my feet lies a soldier as flat as a board, like dead. One more spent man, one more grey face.

July 23, 1945

It might be the twenty-second. Who knows? Who cares in this hell?

We are in the city of Halle, again on the railway platform. It's a big city. Thousands of us wait for that one train. We are one with the mob. Miserable, hungry, poor, and most in rags. Sick, putrefying, and waiting.

Instead of the expected train, a single steam engine rolled up with a shrill steam whistle buzzing and whistling in our ears for one hour. The right tune for misery.

I discovered a sand mound and crawled up to it (a remnant from the war). I threw myself onto the sand. Couldn't stand up anymore. Linda stayed at its foot with Georg and baggage.

And the hours passed. We exchanged places, room on the pile for only one person. Five hours passed when a train, dark and long, approached, crawling.

Now, help us God. The mob began to move. The human knot around us crushed forward. We grabbed the carriage and all, pushed it up the sand mound which barely held us, while thousands furiously pressed to that black moving thing, screaming wildly, kicking, tearing at each other, hanging onto handles, banging onto doors of a train. It was overcrowded already, might perhaps have had room for twenty more, never thousands.

I watched that train for our chance. There, up at the first coupes. There was no crowd up there, only soldiers with golden decorations. I grabbed Georg and dashed forward. Linda followed with our things. The mob didn't follow, stopped as by an invisible wall. I looked at Russian soldiers' faces and glimpsed the "Reserved Military Compartment" signs on all the doors.

"Theatre, theatre. I am an actress," I stammered over and over again. Somehow, I knew that these words would be understood. Russians understand theatre and stage actors.

They let us in. There was room and we could sit down. I could change Georg and give him his juice. And the train moved.

From out of nowhere and with grinning faces, the Russians produced a bottle of vodka. One of them, holding a dictionary in his hand, searched for the words, *glass* then *Tasse* (cup). I gave him the baby cup. They all laughed and filled it and passed it around. And we all drank from it.

We talked and talked. What? How? I don't know. We couldn't understand each other, but there was a kind of friendship. A mother and her little one had been helped, and these soldiers were happy to have helped.

The train came to a final stop in Bitterfeld. We got out and thanked our strange Russian soldiers.

Once more thrown into the middle of the stream, the misery stream to Berlin. Must keep above water, find shelter. Find food. We must. No concern, no eyes for others, only for ourselves. Too tired to talk. Swept along with the mob we learned to use our elbows, had to. We had to get clear, but how? Thousands around us, with us, with sacks, cartons, children. Just as burdened and hungry as we.

Pushing along the streets, pushing forward to the same goals: a place for the night and food. One harried, stinking mass.

Stay above them, try to stay up higher, hammered into my being. And never go to into the mass-quarters. Never. If we must, stay out in the open field in the night.

When approaching the first quarters, a bunker, haggard adults carried out dead children, one after the other. Whoever we asked where to find shelter, to whomever we turned for help or directions, hurried away without even looking at us. They didn't know, or, if they did, kept that to themselves.

Linda? We never would have made it without her. She sat on some ruin-wall with Georg while I tried the mayor of the city of Bitterfeld.

27

An Old Nazi Estate

After hours of searching, elbows, and the right words, I found the mayor of Bitterfeld's house. He gave me a permit to occupy a room in a villa evacuated by a once famous Nazi industrialist.

I am now sitting here in this villa, writing.

My son is outside in his carriage in a garden again, trees again. A time to recover. His diapers flutter in the wind and sun. A time to breathe again. Carrots and potatoes were for sale in the city without ration stamps. I am not hungry for the first time in a long, long time.

The villa's furniture is gone. We sit on the floor and sleep on the floor.

Oh yes, for Georg there is a basket-Betti. He can stretch out. The owner must have forgotten it or could not lug it to where he fled. God looks out for us again. There is a big kitchen and some wood to boil potatoes and heat water. There are some kitchen utensils and a pail to wash and do our laundry.

All rooms, halls, and cellar are occupied. Freed prisoners of war on their treks through the Reich, wounded soldiers, all of them resting before continuing their walk home. And children, many children of all ages, and all without any parent. The woman who let us in, the housekeeper, watches over them, cares for them.

No one here in the villa talks much. Too tired. Too worried, nothing worth the energy it takes to talk.

The housekeeper did tell me briefly about the children here, children whose parents died at the Zone crossing, right here at the Mulde River, drowned or shot.

In recent days, the Mulde marked the boundary between the American and Russian Zones. When the Russians arrived, they shut it off overnight and kept it shut after they occupied the region down to Stutzhaus and beyond. But thousands of people were on the trek, as we are now, and suddenly could go no farther.

They had to press on, to find shelter, to find husband, relatives, father, mother, home, something to eat. They wanted to cross that river and flee the Russians while they still could. At night or far from the guards, they tried to cross the Mulde.

There's a village up at the Mulde's shore, about fifteen kilometers from here. At that village, people got the deadly chance to cross, by barge, canoe, raft, anything floating. This little village gets rich on money and on countless nameless graves. Many gave everything of value they had for this one chance to cross the Mulde into the American zone.

Except for the few hours when the river border was opened, Russian guards searched the water at night with floodlights. They shot at boats and everyone in them with machine guns. That's why these children are here and alone.

Now the Zone is open. The Russians occupy both sides of the river but let some people cross and through.

We'll have to walk these fifteen kilometers to the crossing point. Then we might have to wait. No one knows when the Russians are willing to open the crossing, sometimes only twice a week.

A few hundred may cross over on the small temporary bridge. But thousands wait, sleep in the trampled fields, dig out potatoes, eat them raw until chased out by farmers with sticks. All are possessed by the force of survival, of finding their loved ones at any price. Just as possessed as we.

The Zone is open now, but no one knows for how long, when the Russians will close it again, when the temporary bridge will break. Everyone here bears the chaos, the hunger, the cold nights, the miserable aftermath. A few leave to not return.

I will go to the river crossing, alone first, to observe and learn what I am able.

We were on the road from Gotha to this villa in Bitterfeld for six days and nights, one hundred and sixty kilometers. In peacetime the train makes it in ninety minutes. And men fly around the globe in four days.

But what do I want? My son has a bed again, and it is white and clean. I could even give him a bath in a new child's tub left behind.

July 24, 1945

Still in Bitterfeld. My feet are too swollen. My thoughts slow and heavy and grey, like lead.

Is anyone still alive in Berlin, friends we will need so urgently? Can we survive hunger much longer?

What irony. I still have cans and bags with food for my boy, but he must starve. That last doctor in Gotha said not to give him anything but water and sugar for a while longer. A few times, a Good

Samaritan gave me milk for the baby, and the baby couldn't have it. I drank it greedily. In Halle we tried to see a doctor, waited three hours, in vain. Too many sick. Back to the train station. Must keep moving forward.

Yet Georg is in rather good spirits, only so terribly tired and weak. Where is his happy kicking, his fidgeting and storytelling?

Our Papa? If I can find a trace in our winter nest in Kladow, or at the address where we said we would meet? But first we must get there.

I must write of that violent hailstorm yesterday, a witch's cauldron. Thunder, lightning, furious howling and raging outside. An incredible uproar. I again pushed Georg in his basket Betti into the farthest corner of the room here in the old villa. I expected our house walls to be blown open. I prayed aloud. After ten minutes it was over.

Icy air, icy quiet. All windows broken. Huge trees splintered like matches. The streets white, covered by egg-sized hailstones, fruit trees in the garden shredded, vegetables mashed, the earth steamed. The storm killed many, and I thanked God that He kept us from having to wait in the fields and helped us to this shelter.

July 27, 1945

Tomorrow the first train will go over the bridges, cross the Elbe, cross the Mulde. Now we must get onto that train here in Bitterfeld at the railroad station.

The soldiers here in the villa talk about it too, but they advise waiting. "The temporary bridges might not hold up," they all say.

The soldiers: Usually they lie on the floor in the hall all day and night and sleep and sleep. When awake they help in the house, cut

186

wood for the kitchen stove, keep the fire going so I'm able to cook meager soups and have good warm water for his bath. They help the many children with no parents. Today they are busy cleaning up the hailstorm damage in the garden and around the house.

Linda has become our good friend. Love made her leave with us. Her man is already in Berlin. Her little girl is safe and secure back in Stutzhaus with the grandparents, but... she worries about collecting her once the Russians clasp hold of the region. They are still letting people in and out of the Stutzhaus region, but no one is sure for how much longer. The Americans and British allow civilians to move freely but not the Russians.

July 28, 1945

I was in the city to inquire about the train.

The train is going, but the Russian commandant does not yet give out any permits to cross over to Berlin. Went to the railroad station to try to buy tickets as one might have long ago. In vain, no tickets yet. But the train sat there at the station, waiting like the rest of us. Well, then we shall go without tickets. We'll find a way.

We prepare for the journey. I negotiate with the housekeeper for the basket-Betti. It has little wooden wheels, which might be of great help. Ours was left behind in Stutzhaus, and surely nothing like this will be left in Berlin. I pay her a hundred marks, though it really does not belong to her either. In peacetime it would have cost fifteen.

28

Last Train Ride

July 29, 1945

We are on the road, on the misery street again, with the mob, lugging and pushing and waiting and hungry and all of us dirty.

As in calmest peacetime, a city street-cleaning official in full official-looking uniform swept the street in front of our villa. It was early, a little after five in the morning but already in early daylight.

Linda and I climbed over the sleeping soldiers in the hall with carriage, basket, bags, and suitcases. No one paid attention to our leaving.

If not for the barrowman, we would still be standing in front of the villa. When he saw us with our loads, he tipped over his wheelbarrow filled with wilted leaves, loaded up our luggage, and wheeled us away over to the railroad station. Then, behind the station building he wheeled our freight right to the train. We didn't need tickets, and no barrier stopped us. Our newest guardian angel piloted us over broken wires, broken bricks and holes, over railroad tracks right to the train.

A Russian sentry nearby looked on. He must have thought the

street sweeper (in uniform with a bright cap) was an official of a rank at least as high as his.

The train was rather empty, and we found seats.

After three hours of waiting and wondering, the train moved over the Mulde, over the Elbe, snail-like, but it kept moving for eight hours to the next big city, Wittenberg, made famous by Martin Luther. We arrived late in the afternoon. We had nothing but carrots, so I had to feed Georg like a cow feeds her young, with chewed carrots.

Then it started all over again. Begging and wandering from house to house for a place for the night. Nothing. Many door signs said, "TYPHUS." From store to store to find something to eat. Nothing. Not even for ration stamps.

Late in the evening at a butchery, a friendly butcher gave us some *Blutwurst* (blood sausage).

We rested in a dirty *Kafehaus*. I bedded Georg on a greasy plush sofa and cleaned and changed him. A band of five old men drearily fiddled some old hit. Russian soldiers paid for their cups of corn-coffee with 50-Mark notes.

Georg's sickness pains us. And no place for the night. Nowhere.

We wandered and wandered the streets with our loads.

It has been dark for a long time, and now it is getting cold too. If we don't find shelter, my son won't be able to keep up. Then I would have sacrificed him on the misery street. As I thought these thoughts, we stood in the pitch-black night in front of a church, next to it the parish. I went to the parish.

The minister gave me a scrap of paper with "Marktgasee 8" scribbled on it.

We found it, and there we could spend the night. There I could give my boy a bath, and he could sleep in a clean white bed. Our hostess, another kind old lady, allowed us to heat the Blutwurst and gave us potatoes. In the morning when we departed for the train to Berlin, she graced Georg with a beautiful handmade lace coat.

In Berlin I will find a good doctor who will get my darling well. That will be my first mission.

When my son reads this, he shall be healthy and strong, and he shall never again have to go such roads as in this year, his first year on this earth.

August 9, 1945–Berlin

My dear little boy, a Jewish children's doctor saved your life.

He was shocked. "Your son is starving to death," he said. "Let him eat, eat whatever you can get for him." The doctor back in Gotha was mistaken, or I was mistaken in what he said, in how long Georg had to starve to settle his insides.

We have found a roof, even a balcony high above the ruin-canyons. Our trek Angel's aunt is alive and in good spirits, her home survived only slightly damaged.

We are staying not far from Berlin's center, the area called Charlottenburg, in a big building with a room all to ourselves. When I run out to search and barter, someone is always here to watch over Georg.

The peculiar eccentricity of this war.

Frau Holm, Linda's aunt, young-looking, attractive, spent the Berlin war days almost entirely in her apartment and at the end in the cellar in the same house. "I'd rather die here," she said.

Many of her friends went to bunkers or the subway for shelter and never came back up or become deathly sick.

She runs here and there, always bartering. Her beautiful jewelry goes bit by bit.

"Food is more important now," she says cheerfully and shares with us whatever she brings home. Fat, sugar, flour. She even gave each of us two dollars, which she got for a ring. Two dollars. A fortune. These two dollars are worth more than all my dwindling bundles of marks.

Georg gulps his first real food in many days. He won't stop eating anything I offer, and his blue eyes look at me in puzzlement. I cursed that doctor in Gotha. He also cut his first tooth.

I curse myself for taking the Gotha doctor's instructions too seriously or too literally, for not trusting myself.

We have found another new friend from overseas, who brings the most precious things: oranges, milk powder, egg powder. Every day he brings Georg a health-gift. He is Tom, Linda's Ami from Stutzhaus who got transferred to Berlin.

The city of Berlin smells of ashes and burned buildings, a penetrating, strong odor everywhere. The once mighty city an ocean of ruins, sick, stinking like a dead dragon. It lies at our feet while Georg, high above on the balcony, catches up on sunbeams, on food, and on his happy story-telling, and now and again his shouting for joy.

My heart is glad, the ring around it not so tight.

But now I must write of this last stretch of our journey.

Our final train, the one from Wittenberg to Berlin, stopped far outside the city. We stood at the open field with all our belongings surrounded by hundreds of people, all wanting to reach the city at any price (for whatever they could offer), and as soon as possible.

As usual, Linda carried the basket-Betti filled with blankets and bags while I held the carriage with one hand and with the other hand steadied two suitcases on the carriage.

We spotted a taxicab, to which the crowd swarmed like bees. Many, those who could, haggled about the price. I joined in, and we got it for the highest bid, five hundred marks. How good that I rescued that money bundle in the aftermath. I should have taken out all of it. No banks or money are left. The taxi took us to Linda's aunt's place, and her aunt was home.

29

Old Haunts

The M's: Two girls, pale, thin, and big-eyed, opened the door and let me in. I'm not sure how old they are, hard to tell from their condition. They could be eleven or fifteen, and I don't remember how old they were when last I saw them. I don't dare ask, any answer too painful. In dual monotones, they told me what happened.

Their mother, a painter and writer, lies in a mass grave. The girls don't know where.

In the last days of this war, a "*Stalinorgel*" tore both her legs off. That's a horrible, common name here. I get cold when I hear that word now. It's an evil Russian weapon, a row of rocket launchers carried on a giant truck trailer. For weeks, the Russians fired the rockets into Berlin from those trucks.

The girls barter their priceless collection of porcelain to stay alive.

The T's: Arnold, Mr. T, a director, fell in close combat on the *Halensee Brüke*. That's a little bridge in a residential area near where we are now. Martha, Frau T, bends over her four-year-old daughter, a nearly lifeless skeleton, as though wanting to guard her from further evil. The child is plagued by hunger and typhus.

Over the last year, mother and daughter took shelter underground in the subway tunnel with thousands of others. Near the end, stinking muddy sewage water pushed into the tunnel, rising higher until up to their necks. Above them the battle of Berlin raged. All exits out of the tunnels were choked with rubble. They tried to flee the water, to reach some exit. Martha and her child waded through the tunnel for six kilometers, from the Anhalter subway station to the Stettiner station.

I offered her a little bag of sugar, all I had with me. She cried and while crying made her daughter a *Zuckerstulle*—a piece of black bread sprinkled with sugar.

We must thank God that we made it, that my son is better and can eat again, that we still have food-cans for him which we lugged with us from Kladow to Stutzhaus and back to Berlin. Those cans are our gold. I still have a ring to barter for food if I need to.

L. W.: My dearest friend and a colleague—dead. Bombs. She was young, beautiful, cherished by all who knew her.

Bill Postings: On broken walls, fences, tree stumps. Colorful paper-slips, notes, some red, some green. They are all the same.

"Help me find my three children . . . last seen . . . "

"My husband . . . last seen . . . "

"Give diamond ring for bicycle . . . please contact . . . "

"A new dress for bacon fat or butter . . . I live at . . . "

"Radio, meat and money for bicycle . . . Please find me in . . . "

A bicycle has the greatest value, as much as an old car that needs petrol and could break down anywhere with no parts to fix it.

I too rode a bike through the city for a day, through heaps of rubble, to find vegetables, any food, to look for friends whose houses and streets no longer exist. I paid an enormous sum to borrow this bike and bartered two dresses for one pound of flour, one pound of margarine, and a bit of coffee, 150 grams.

A huge tank sat in the middle of Kurfürstendamm. Its tread lay a hundred meters away. A screaming, yellow placard on the tank said: CABARET!

On almost every street corner a "Theatre" has sprung up, featuring names unknown but in giant letters.

Now and again, like a bright poisonous mushroom, a well-groomed, well-dressed woman walks the streets.

Every day I course through this ruin-giant on foot (can't afford the bike anymore), over hills of debris, carefully balance my way over narrow boards and look and search and ask. I look bearded soldiers in the face. They don't mind. Everyone does that.

At the ration stamp issuing office, I met a colleague of Papa. He said that he saw him during the last days of the war. That he saw him at a distance though. Doubt... hope... so close. Where, I don't know. But I must keep looking, must stay alert.

I've learned that as soon as I have work, I'll go into "Group Two." That means twice the ration stamps, a privilege for actors.

August 28, 1945

I must find work. Our money will soon be gone. Prices rise fifty percent every day. I can sing. I'll work in a cabaret. It doesn't matter where I work.

Georg looks so much like his father.

Yet we are lucky still. A man who owns a truck lives downstairs. He delivers potatoes. He has brought us a bag two times already and offered to take me along when he drives to Kladow tomorrow.

I might find a message in one of our so painstakingly nailed wooden boxes and crates. Perhaps Papa waited for us in Kladow. Hope.

August 30, 1945

It was late when I returned from Kladow yesterday. My darling was asleep, sound asleep and healthy-looking. I sat next to him for a long time, deeply grateful.

In Kladow, I embraced our little apartment house, and those near. Many houses stood looking undisturbed in rows, enshrouded by meadows and trees and yellow early autumn leaves dancing in the breeze. But the bomb craters remained, ugly and painful the memories.

At our former apartment, a strange woman surrounded by children opened the door. I counted four but heard more.

"Frau I. (our landlady) never made it," the woman said. "All of them killed somewhere on their flight from the east of Berlin, on their way here." She did not say how she knew, and I did not ask. Makes no difference. Frau I. would be here if she were alive.

I asked the stranger if a man came by here, asked about his wife and son. The woman understood and shook her head.

She opened the cellar for me to get to our boxes and crates. They were there, all of them, but all of them empty, filled with rubbish, straw, even Hitler pictures. Too tired, too sad, to get angry. It's just that today every dish and pan, every blanket is so very precious.

I rummaged through that trash, through every piece of straw to perhaps still find a message. Nothing.

I went over to the other rows of houses, to our neighbor, the lady with the two daughters, who had to sacrifice the remaining clothes of her fallen husband to the Nazis. We embraced and cried. She shared her coffee ration with me, and slowly we began to speak.

She looks quite radiant, I thought, and learned she'll get married to a British soldier. Yes, the English occupy this section out there. May God bless her future.

And we? We easily could have stayed right there to await the end, to wait for our landlady and her family to return without notice. We could have spared ourselves so much. Who knew, who would have guessed? No time or purpose in looking back.

The truck owner must have read my thoughts. On our way to Berlin, he promised to take me along when he next drives to Nauen, the town where our uncle and aunt found shelter before we left. "Maybe you'll find them," he said. How he knew I wanted to go there is a puzzle. I must have blurted out more of my story on the ride to Kladow. I'm more forgetful now.

30

Other Survivors

September 3, 1945

Meats of different kinds, real coffee, and cake. There was a sparkling engagement ring too. Georg beamed and laughed at Tom and Linda as though he wholeheartedly approved. I cried. I still cry too easily.

Tom also brought the sounds of the world, a battery-powered radio. "The latest," he said.

Amazed, we stared at this wonder. While others developed magnificent things, we destroyed. I am bitter, but that shall pass.

Another surprise and gladness. A voice on the radio, then the name on Radio Berlin, a commentary by Fred Meyer.

I couldn't speak for a long time, thoughts about our work in the theatre, how fast he had to leave then for Switzerland. That was the last we knew of him, and now his voice . . .

Das *Rundfukhaus*, Berlin's broadcast station, is not too far from here, an hour's walk perhaps. It was spared from the bombs and rockets. Tomorrow we shall go there.

What an evening. Peace. Love and signs of a future of peace.

I'll take some of our good food to Martha and her little daughter.

September 4, 1945

We saw Fred, but one thing after another.

I took Georg along in the carriage. The broken wheels have been fixed, for bread ration stamps new spokes. We managed to roll through broken streets, over rubble heaps, to the Rundfunkhaus.

It stood big and almost untouched and so familiar. How often I entered that building, usually in a hurry between theatre rehearsals and parts or interviews on radio shows. I felt strange now standing there again in front of the wide stairs up to the entrance. With a son, swept by a war, and on my search.

I had never raised my right arm in salute. One absolutely had to raise the right arm in the Hitler salute when entering the celebrated Funkhaus, the most important broadcasting station in the Third Reich. It felt like a deadly game, each time I kept my arm down. No one ever yelled out, ever admonished me. Perhaps the SS sentries thought me stupid or the kept woman of someone important. Now instead of the SS man an American sentry guards the entrance.

We couldn't drive in with carriage, but the sentry let me leave the carriage with him after I explained who we came to see. My English has gotten better from talking with Tom. I took Georg in my arms to Fred's office.

Fred didn't recognize me, that momentary hesitation when the mind tried to match memory of the past and the present. I must look awful compared to back then. He tried not to show it.

He had flown in from New York only two weeks before, he said, and made it out of Switzerland to America in time. The Nazis even looked for him in Switzerland.

I lost all poise and cried and became dizzy. After some cognac or whatever, calmed down. "Flying" from "New York," while we?

That new world is out there. It waits for us.

Georg behaved wonderfully, looked around as though he understood everything.

Now, as I write this, I hear Fred's encouraging words, and his suggestion to start work on the radio. He will come to us tomorrow and might be able to help me find a radio spot.

How we got home I don't know. An hour's walk seemed to take minutes.

Elated? Hope? There might be work for me, and I have found a friend. My heart still aches, even more now and every day with no sign of him. But then, if we could find Fred from far away, why shouldn't we find my husband?

September 6, 1945

Seems all good spirits are busy helping us up onto our feet again.

Fred came by and filled our table with precious things: Milk powder, bread, cans of meat, sugar, bacon fat, flour, some cognac. And even baby clothes. I was elated and still am.

Fred told me about a mutual friend.

Kl, a famous actor, art collector, and humanitarian. Loyal to his principles, he never joined the Nazi party, as good a man in life as up there on stage.

When the Russians arrived and occupied sections of Berlin, many of them swept into undamaged neighborhoods where cowering civilians rode out the war. Russians went marauding for vengeance and raped undefended women, then shot everyone alive. When they rang the doorbell at Kl's house, he politely opened—and they shot him dead on the spot.

31

September 14, 1945

It's night now, three in the morning. But I no longer need to steal a moment's time.

The trek, our search, our own war, are ended, and . . . We have won.

Our greatest day began early yesterday morning. The potato truck had to leave for Nauen on short notice. At about six there was a knock on the door to our room.

"Sorry, it's so early, but I thought you would like to come along with me," said Mr. Huber, the truck owner.

I left Georg with Linda.

At sunrise, I stood in front of an unknown church and parish in the village of Nauen. I asked Mr. Huber not to wait. I wanted to be alone no matter what I found. He left and promised to pick me up at noon.

Red rays of the rising sun covered the earth, and the world smelled of wet grass and blossoms. Peace. I prayed with all my heart that I would find our uncle and aunt, that they would be alive and not harmed too badly by the rest of their journey.

After a long time of just standing, turning, watching the sun come up, letting it warm me, I found the courage to knock on the heavy door of the parish house.

Uncle Bruno opened it. My voice choked, tears streamed without end.

He led me into the house, gesturing as though I were something or someone very special. "Now everything will be all right," he said.

Then I spotted . . . a man sitting in the corner.

"Oh, my God," I thought or whispered to myself. "*Zertruemert, zertruemert* (shattered, traumatized)."

I couldn't move. He looked at me, lifeless or in a trance. He blinked, and smiled, barely smiled, and reached out a thin, scratched hand. Papa, my husband, my man.

After a time, I realized he couldn't get up.

Later Uncle Bruno said that this morning was the first time, since crawling to the front door, that his brother attempted to be out of bed.

Falling to my knees I buried myself in him and held his hands. How long we embraced I don't know.

Words would have hurt.

Oh, this war! Broken, a broken man, just as the soldiers on the train, just as the soldiers who came hobbling out of dusk in Stutzhaus. The damned of war. One more here. The face, a grey patch. The body, a skeleton. Flickering eyes, stammering.

He uttered only one word, "Georg."

And I said, "We are all right. We love you." I said it again and again.

When the time came for me to leave, he was back in bed and asleep.

I was heavy with worry, but a fog had lifted. I could see the road ahead, our road. He was alive, and the war is over, and we have time. Time, the great healer.

There is love.

I learned about Father's and Bruno's and Maria's recent days.

My husband must have been *verschütert* (buried alive) somewhere near the Russian front in Berlin, struggled mightily to find his way to light and out, and then he too wandered, his shoes in tatters, his feet bleeding. One morning an unconscious man lay at the parish's doorstep, and his brother, Uncle Bruno, carried him in.

The Russians swept through this area soon after. Here too in Nauen the Russians went from house to house and shot anyone they saw, shot any man who opened the door. Uncle Bruno opened the door to find a young Russian soldier with a gun pointed at him.

"I was not afraid. I looked him straight in the eye, and then I blessed him in Russian. He didn't shoot."

Aunt Maria is pale and stutters a bit. She had to give herself to three Russian soldiers.

———————————

So much to do.

Frau Holm said she will put an extra bed in our room to have all three of us together. In a week or so, he can be moved.

I'll ask Fred to help get him medicine; he needs special medicine. We will get that too. I have those dresses to barter. Soon we'll get extra ration stamps, so much to love. Daddy is alive! We have survived, all of us. He will get well. We will find a place to live together once more.

And when he sees his son . . .

November 3, 1945

Two months have passed, and I haven't found time to write.

But TODAY, on the third day of November, on our son's first birthday, I must report on how it has been and is now with the three of us.

A short while after I visited Nauen, Daddy was able to leave and come home with us. Fred and I drove him to Berlin.

Fred. Through him, we got Father on his feet. Fred found our transportation, hard to get medicine, then food, and constant encouragement. Our son, our dear boy, smiled away ailments and worries, stretched out his arms toward his Papa and so often shouted for joy.

Frau Holm helped us find another apartment with some furniture, also here in Charlottenburg, a noble lady.

We have two rooms and share the kitchen with the owner. The living room ceiling is adorned by a long black pipe, in many parts and sections. It starts at a little iron stove in our room and winds through the room and out the window, all built with care and a bit of pain by Papa.

How we got these pipes and lifesaving stove is a story of its own.

We searched and cross-bartered for weeks.

For many bread stamps, sugar.

For sugar and cigarettes, one piece of pipe.

For a beautiful evening coat of mine, the curved pipe that leads out through the window.

For dollars! (from Fred again), the old stove.

Before the war, this house had been heated by central heat from the basement.

Today I am more excited than in a long time. At eight in the morning, we, Mommy and Daddy, brought a birthday cake to our son's Betti. One candle burned in the middle. And on the birthday table we set little flags of many nations. The whole world for our son. And five red apples!

Later

Little right hand in Mommy's left hand, little left hand in Daddy's right hand, baby tiptoed across the room. Happiness. And another white tooth has emerged.

Father and Fred will attend the theatre tonight. We even got a babysitter. They will take blankets along as will everyone else. No coals yet. But it will always be crowded, because it is a happy play, and laughter warms too.

Wrapped in a glistening gown, I will sing a song of Love and The Sea. Grace to embrace my beloved theatre again. So soon.

Linda and Tom will be there. They will soon marry and then leave for America. The Russians are still too disorganized and miserable and trying to get what they can from the British and Americans. Hence, they too allow civilians to move between occupied regions. Linda and Tom will go to America with their daughter and maybe Linda's mom too. A gracious and lovely woman, who shared her bed with me outside a war-torn village in Germany, will fly to the mighty United States and become an American bride.

Late the next day while all was quiet and Georg in his playpen played enthralled with Papa's pipe, he said, "What might he want to become someday?"

I said, "He? He is probably one of the men who will first fly to the Moon. If he wants to become a shoemaker or a pianist, it really makes no difference . . . so long as he is happy. Our disaster. That youth had been forced into ideologies imposed by our rulers, into professions heaped on them by others.

"The most natural traits of children became torpid, their characters constrained, their lives twisted into ways wrong for them and all around them. Force and pressure rule their lives. To what end? A singular monstrous misadventure, misery and affliction."

With a free yawn, our son stopped these grandiose words, and we got ready to put him to bed. I took him into my arms while Papa folded the playpen and we both kissed him goodnight.

Then I said his *Abendgebet* (Evening prayer).

Müde bin ich geh zur Ruh.
Schliesse meine Augen zu
Vater lass die Augen Dein
Über Meinem Bette Sein
Alle Menschen gross end klein
Sollen Dir empfolen sein
Kranke Herzen sende Ruh
Nasse Augen schliesse zu
Lass den Mond am Himmel stehn
Und kein Wanderer irre gehn.

(Tired I am and go to rest/Close my eyes/Father, let Thine eyes/Be over my bed/May all people big and small/Be in Thy care/Send peace to the sick at heart/Close wet eyes/Let the Moon stand in the Sky/And let no wanderer go astray.)

UND LASS NIE WIEDER KRIEG SEIN
AND LET THERE NEVER AGAIN BE WAR

Katharina and son Georg
have survived.

This is a true story. Some names have been changed and details of some personal relationships changed to protect the privacy of those still living and their loved ones.

Through it all, Katharina managed to save and hang onto news clippings and photos from some of her performances. These were later compiled into Volume 1 and Volume 2, then digitized, with some of the photos remastered to appear glossy and original.

The cover photo, taken in the Fall of 1937, shows Katharina after she had just turned twenty-seven. The deprivations of war had not yet begun. Make-up artists, costume designers for German stage and movie productions thrived.

The photo introducing Part 1, taken in early 1941, shows Katharina as Lady Milford in Shiller's *Kabale und Liebe (Cabal and Love)*. The play ran in the prestigious Frankfurter Stadttheater.

The photo leading into Part 2, taken in November 1941, shows Katharina in the role of Aimée from Heinz Coubier's *Aimée or Common Sense*. This comedy was performed in the Aachen Stadttheater, with another Katharina photo featured on the cover of the show's playbill. The burdens on civilians in war shows starkly when compared to the cover photo of just four years earlier.

Part 3 is headed by an undated photo on the very last page of Katharina's Scrapbook, Volume 2.

The image at the beginning of Part 4 is from a July 1938 magazine feature article on "The Actress Katharina Berger."

The photo on the previous page shows Katharina and her son Georg, survivors of World War II. For some months now, they have found enough to eat. She has found work.

ACKNOWLEDGMENTS

Every day I give thanks to my mother, Katharina, for bringing me into this life and keeping me alive during my first year. I give thanks for her strength, wisdom, and integrity. I give thanks to her spirit that allows me to now, almost eighty years later, share her story of that harrowing time and place.

I marvel that she stole moments of time to record details of daily life before they became smothered and lost in the fog and tumult of history. I stand in awe that she kept those notes, along with news clippings and photos from her stunning career cut short. She not only lugged them with her while fleeing from place to place during World War II, but then kept them intact for years until she could compile them into two scrapbooks and organize the notes into a diary form manuscript.

I am deeply grateful to the Greatest Generation of Americans for taking on and defeating Hitler, for helping to rebuild and not oppress conquered lands, for treating defenseless civilians honorably. From care packages delivered to us when I was a small boy, I remember what we called "red pudding," strawberry Jell-O, and I love it still. I appreciate so much the generosity of Americans back then and at every step in my life.

I thank *New York Times* and *USA Today* bestselling fiction author Kim Michele Richardson, who had also penned her own biography, for believing in this project, for catching little nits and a few bigger ones in the manuscript that needed fixing, and for answering my every question.

I appreciate Acorn Publishing and its team, their competence and responsiveness. Co-founder Holly Kammier brings a delightful intensity to her authors' works. My main Acorn contact, Jessica Hammett, does not let an e-mail or phone message go unanswered and keeps me informed every step of the way. Acorn has superb editors and typesetters and helps create stunning covers. Acorn not only agreed to publish this memoir but did so without changing a single word—so that I and others can say this is truly Katharina's memoir.

I am blessed on my journey with a wonderful life partner, Virginia, our two sons and their families. We all deeply appreciate my Mom's heroic pursuit of Life.

G. J. Berger
San Diego, CA, August 2023

Made in United States
North Haven, CT
24 June 2024